CW01021186

HIDDEN REPRESSION

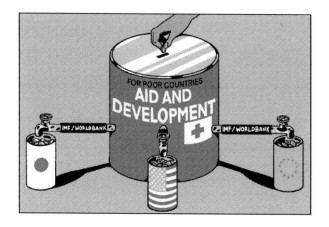

HIDDEN REPRESSION

ALEX GLADSTEIN

Bitcoin Magazine Books
Nashville, TN.

A version of this content was originally published in *Bitcoin Magazine*.

ISBN 979-8-9876363-9-8 – (hardcover)
ISBN 979-8-9876364-0-4 – (ebook)

Published by Bitcoin Magazine Books
An imprint of BTC Media, LLC
438 Houston St. #257 Nashville, TN 37203 Address all inquiries to contact@btcmedia.org

Printed by Amazon
Formatting by RMK Publications, LLC
Aid and Development artwork by Duke Nguyen

For the victims of development —

they may never get the justice they deserve,

but they may get a way out.

TABLE OF CONTENTS

Foreword: What If?..1

Author's Note...5

I . The Shrimp Fields 9

II. Inside the World Bank and IMF 15

III. Structural Adjustment..23

IV. The Debt Trap...31

V. Replacing the Colonial Resource Drain..............................37

VI. A Dance With Dictators 45

VII. Creating Agricultural Dependence.................................57

VIII. You Can't Eat Cotton 63

IX. The Development Set 69

X. White Elephants...77

XI. A Real-Life Pandora: The Exploitation of West Papua 83

XII. The World's Biggest Ponzi 91

XIII. Do as I Say, Not as I Do 97

XIV. Green Colonialism..101

XV. The Human Toll of Structural Adjusment 107

XVI. A Trillion Dollars: The Bank and Fund in the Post-Covid World 113

XVII. From Arusha to Accra 121

XVIII. A Glimmer of Hope 129

Recommended Reading 139

Afterword: Hope for the Colonized 143

About the Author 147

Endnotes 149

WHAT IF?

What if you were one of the relatively small number of people on this planet that benefited from the same economic system that *required* billions of people on the planet to be sacrificed?

Rather than investigate an ugly truth on its merit, perhaps it would be easier to ignore, or tell yourself that there was nothing you could do.

What if you were one of the billions?

Depending on what side of the equation you're on, this existential question underlies all our choices and range of outcomes as we transition from a global economic system requiring manipulation of money to an economic system without manipulation.

The debt that underlies our economies is insolvent. Without adding for unfunded liabilities, that global debt is approaching $400 trillion and growing exponentially, especially in the Global South. That growing debt is our way of life, and we have become trapped in it continuing to grow because the existing system would collapse if the technologically led productivity gains were allowed to flow to society in the form of lower prices.

Why? Because if prices were to fall consistently as technology allowed society to get more for less, the already insolvent debt would rise in real terms and default, creating a deflationary depression as the holders of the debt were wiped out. But when the entire global monetary system is built on that same debt, the administrators cannot allow a system collapse.

As a result, our world is ruled by hypocrisy. We allow the transfer of wealth through the manipulation of money to the creditors (who would otherwise fail) at the expense of billions of people losing their purchasing power. Worse still, those on the winning side of this unfair transfer of wealth rise to top positions within the financial, political, and economic system where they prey on others in the developing world as its people become stuck in a doom loop. So desperate for economic development, they are easily swayed to see the creditors as saviors and take on more debt in the process, which only binds them and makes them poorer.

A systemic problem is difficult to see from within the system, so it is much easier to believe a lie: That inflation (or manipulation of money) is somehow required to live in a productive society. The lie has become so entrenched in society that we take the lie at face value, without asking who wins and who loses from that global theft in money. The outcome is so surreal that we've created a world that requires people to literally gamble on where to place their money to avoid it losing its purchasing power, and then we wonder why our world looks the way it does.

But this lie has consequences that predictably grow worse over time as the money manipulation and the inflation rate must increase to hide the growing debt. The consequences go far beyond getting paid less in real terms for work or losing life savings for large portions of the population. Because money is superordinate to laws, individual rights and freedoms predictably contract as trusted institutions become captured by big money. As they do, societal decay accelerates. Why? Because laws change over time, ensuring those with root access to money, either rewrite the laws, prevail in court, or usurp the laws through revolutions promising change—but ultimately just putting a new face on the systemic problem.

The rule of law doesn't protect citizens from the manipulation of money. It protects those closest to the manipulation.

In other words, the direct consequence to billions of people of a system masquerading as a free market—but built on a theft—is a predictable rise of dictators and modern-day slavery for a majority of the planet's inhabitants.

That so many are trapped in a corrupt system with few good options seems hopeless, until one realizes that a new monetary system is emerging from the outside which allows a transition.

Bitcoin: A permissionless, decentralized, and secure protocol built on rules that remove the ability to manipulate money. At this point, Bitcoin is likely unstoppable, which is a good thing. This exponentially growing, emergent network can eventually transition a system built on misinformation, theft, and coercion to a system built on truth, hope, and freedom. A literal bridge to the other side. Because the new system benefits from powerful network effects, providing more value to *all* participants with each new user of the system, over time, society transitions from a world based on scarcity to a world of abundance.

In reading through Alex's brilliant and comprehensive treatise, you will be investigating the big economic lie of our world at its root: The powerful help the weak. Following that, you will face an important choice.

What system do you choose?

While you contemplate, it is worth remembering that we are all responsible for the world we want to see.

Choose wisely.

—Jeff Booth

Author, *Price of Tomorrow*,
and General Partner, Ego Death Capital

Author's Note

Writing this book was a powerful journey. *Hidden Repression* took me from shock, to disbelief, to shame, to optimism for a better future.

I had heard criticisms about the IMF, especially its role in the Global South. I had heard many speak about the World Bank as a necessary but flawed institution.

I was not prepared for what I unearthed.

It is one thing for global institutions to be corrupt, trying to help the poor but failing along the way. It is another thing entirely for the intent of these institutions to be to take from the weak and give to the strong.

We have been sold a lie: that development is to help poor countries. In practice, "development" over the last 50 years has been neocolonial: looting trillions of dollars of resources from the Global South for the Global North, and depressing wages in the developing world to prevent inflation and economic crises from occurring in the West.

This painful truth continues even now, as dozens of economies in the Global South collapse as a result of the US government's attempts to tame domestic inflation by rapidly increasing interest rates. As of the publication of this book, the Western financial system is starting to break because of the

Federal Reserve's decisions. What the media isn't saying is
that those decisions already broke the financial systems that
hundreds of millions of people rely on in developing countries
and dictatorships.

As someone who has spent my career fighting for the
classic Western values of freedom and human rights, this book
has taught me two things. Number one: these values are more
important than ever before and essential for the future success
of humanity. Number two: one cost of securing these
freedoms in the West has been the deprivation of these
freedoms for people elsewhere.

Writing this book made me ask an uncomfortable
question: does democratic capitalism rely on exploitation? We
only have one version of history, in which the West advances
at the expense of the rest.

It also made me think: what is the source of this rot? One
major part of it, I am now convinced, is the fiat currency
system. This is evident when we see the explosion of Third
World debt begin to skyrocket after 1971.

Satoshi Nakamoto set many things in motion with their
creation of Bitcoin. One is a potential future world where no
government can manipulate the reserve currency, and no
world power can simply print money to bail out dictators with
no penalty. This would be an upgrade, even for those of us
who benefit from the system.

The best elements of Western civilization are, in my view,
its core founding values: free speech, independent media,

privacy, separation of powers, civil society, private property, open markets, and rule by the people. The problem is that we have betrayed these values, at home, yes, but much more violently abroad. This betrayal hurts our victims the most, but it also corrupts, wounds, and impairs us at home.

As you read this book, I hope you can join me on my journey in reflecting on history with humility, and my attempt to better understand why some nations have prospered while others have suffered. And I hope you can join me and a growing movement of millions of people across the globe in helping to build a world based on cooperation, not exploitation.

—Alex Gladstein

March 2023

How the IMF and World Bank Sell Exploitation as Development

I . THE SHRIMP FIELDS

"Everything is gone."

—*Kolyani Mondal*

Fifty-two years ago, Cyclone Bhola killed an estimated 1 million people in coastal Bangladesh.[1] It is, to this day, the deadliest tropical cyclone in recorded history.[2] Local and international authorities knew well the catastrophic risks of such storms: In the 1960s, regional officials had built a massive array of dikes to protect the coastline and open up more territory for farming.[3] But in the 1980s, after the assassination of independence leader Sheikh Mujibur Rahman, foreign influence pushed a new autocratic Bangladeshi regime to change course. Concern for human life was dismissed and the public's protection against storms was weakened, all in order to boost exports to repay debt.

Instead of reinforcing the local mangrove forests which naturally protected one-third of the population that lived near the coast,[4] and instead of investing in growing food to feed the quickly growing nation, the government took out loans from the World Bank[5] and International Monetary Fund (IMF)[6] in order to expand shrimp farming. The aquaculture process— controlled by a network of wealthy elites linked to the regime—involved pushing farmers to take out loans to "upgrade" their operations by drilling holes in the dikes that protected their land from the ocean, filling their once-fertile fields with saltwater.[7] Then, they would work backbreaking hours to hand-harvest young shrimp from the ocean, drag them back to their stagnant ponds, and sell the mature ones to the local shrimp lords.

With financing from the World Bank and IMF, countless farms and their surrounding wetlands and mangrove forests were engineered into shrimp ponds known as *ghers*.[8] The area's Ganges River delta is an incredibly fertile place, home to the Sundarbans, the world's biggest stretch of mangrove forest. [9] But as a result of commercial shrimp farming becoming the region's main economic activity, 45% of the mangroves have been cut away, leaving millions of people exposed to the ten-meter waves that can crash against the coast during major cyclones.[10] Arable land and river life have been slowly destroyed by excess salinity leaking in from the sea. Entire forests have vanished,[11] as shrimp farming has killed much of the area's vegetation, "rendering this once bountiful land into a watery desert."[12]

Source: Al Helal/REACH

A farm in Bangladesh's Khulna province, flooded to make shrimp fields.

The shrimp lords,[13] however, have made a fortune, and shrimp (known as "white gold") has become the country's second-largest export.[14] As of 2014, more than 1.2 million Bangladeshis worked in the shrimp industry, with 4.8 million people indirectly dependent on it, roughly half of the coastal poor.[15] The shrimp collectors, who have the toughest job, make up 50% of the labor force but only see 6% of the profit.[16] Of that labor force, 30% of them are girls and boys engaged in child labor, who work as much as nine hours a day in the salt water, for less than $1 per day, with many giving up school and remaining illiterate to do so. Protests against the expansion of shrimp farming have happened, only to be put down violently. In one prominent case, a march was attacked with explosives from shrimp lords and their thugs, and a woman named Kuranamoyee Sardar was decapitated.[17]

In a 2007 research paper, 102 Bangladeshi shrimp farms were surveyed, revealing that, out of a cost of production of $1,084 per hectare, the net income was $689.[18] The nation's export-driven profits came at the expense of the shrimp laborers, whose wages were deflated and whose environment was destroyed.

In a report by the Environmental Justice Foundation, a coastal farmer named Kolyani Mondal said that she "used to farm rice and keep livestock and poultry," but after shrimp harvesting was imposed, "her cattle and goats developed diarrhea-type disease and, together with her hens and ducks, all died."[19]

Now her fields are flooded with salt water, and what remains is barely productive: Years ago, her family could generate "18-19 *mon* of rice per hectare," but now they can only generate one. She remembers shrimp farming in her area beginning in the 1980s, when villagers were promised more income as well as lots of food and crops, but now "everything is gone." The shrimp farmers who use her land promised to pay her $140 per year, but she says the best she gets are "occasional installments of $8 here or there." In the past, she says, "the family got most of the things they needed from the land, but now there are no alternatives but going to the market to buy food."

In Bangladesh, billions of dollars of World Bank and IMF "structural adjustment" loans—named for the way they force borrowing nations to modify their economies to favor exports at the expense of consumption—grew national shrimp profits from $2.9 million in 1973 to $90 million in 1986 to $590 million in 2012.[20] As in most cases with developing countries, the revenue was used to service foreign debt, develop military assets, and line the pockets of government officials. As for the shrimp serfs, they have been impoverished: less free, more dependent, and less able to feed themselves than before. To make matters worse, studies show that "villages shielded from the storm surge by mangrove forests experience significantly fewer deaths" than villages which had their protections removed or damaged.[21]

Under public pressure in 2013, the World Bank loaned Bangladesh $400 million to try and reverse the ecological damage.[22] In other words, the World Bank will be paid a fee in the form of interest to try and fix the problem it created in the first place. Meanwhile, the World Bank has loaned billions to countries everywhere from Ecuador[23] to Morocco[24] to India[25] to replace traditional farming with shrimp production.

The World Bank claims that Bangladesh is "a remarkable story of poverty reduction and development."[26] On paper, victory is declared: Countries like Bangladesh tend to show economic growth over time as their exports rise to meet their imports. But exports earnings flow mostly to the ruling elite and international creditors. After ten structural adjustments,[27] Bangladesh's debt pile has grown exponentially from $145 million in 1972[28] to an all-time high of $95.9 billion in 2022.[29] The country faces yet another balance of payments crisis, and in November 2022, agreed to take its eleventh loan from the IMF, this time a $4.5 billion bailout, in exchange for more adjustment.[30] The World Bank and the IMF claim to want to help poor countries, but the clear outcome after more than fifty years of their policies is that nations like Bangladesh are more dependent and indebted than ever before.

During the 1990s, in the wake of the Third World Debt Crisis, there was a swell of global public scrutiny on the World Bank and IMF: critical studies, street protests, and a widespread, bipartisan belief (even in the halls of the U.S. Congress) that these institutions ranged from wasteful to destructive.[31] But this sentiment and focus has largely faded. Today, the World Bank and the IMF manage to keep a low profile in the press. When they do come up, they tend to be written off as increasingly irrelevant, accepted as problematic yet necessary, or even welcomed as helpful.

The reality is that these organizations have impoverished and endangered millions of people; enriched dictators and kleptocrats; and cast human rights aside to generate a multi-trillion-dollar flow of food, natural resources, and cheap labor from poor countries to rich ones. Their behavior in countries like Bangladesh is no mistake or exception: Selling exploitation as "development" is their way of doing business.

II. INSIDE THE WORLD BANK AND IMF

"Let us remember that the main purpose of aid is not to help other nations but to help ourselves."

—*Richard Nixon*

The IMF is the world's international lender of last resort, and the World Bank is the world's largest development bank.[32] Their work is carried out on behalf of their major creditors, which historically, have been the United States, the United Kingdom, France, Germany, and Japan.[33]

Source: World Bank

The IMF and World Bank offices in Washington, DC.

The sister organizations—physically joined together at their headquarters in Washington, DC—were created at the Bretton Woods Conference in New Hampshire in 1944 as two pillars of the new U.S.-led global monetary order. Per tradition, the World Bank is headed by an American, and the IMF by a European.[34]

Their initial purpose was to help rebuild war-torn Europe and Japan, with the World Bank to focus on specific loans for development projects, and the IMF to address balance-of-payment issues via "bailouts" to keep trade flowing even if countries couldn't afford more imports.

Nations are required to join the IMF in order to get access to the "perks" of the World Bank. Today, there are 190 member states: Each one deposited a mix of their own currency plus "harder currency" (typically dollars, European currencies, or gold) when they joined, creating a pool of reserves.[35]

When members encounter chronic balance-of-payments issues, and cannot make loan repayments, the IMF offers them credit from the pool at varying multiples of what they initially deposited, on increasingly expensive terms.

The IMF is technically a supranational central bank, as since 1969, it has minted its own currency: The special drawing rights (SDR), whose value is based on a basket of the world's top currencies. Today, the SDR is backed by 45% dollars, 29% euros, 12% yuan, 7% yen, and 7% pounds.[36] The total lending capacity of the IMF today stands at $1 trillion.[37]

Between 1960 and 2008, the IMF largely focused on assisting developing countries with short-term, high-interest-rate loans. Because the currencies issued by developing countries are not freely convertible, they usually cannot be redeemed for goods or services abroad. Developing states must instead earn hard currency through exports. Unlike the United States, which can simply issue the global reserve currency, countries like Sri Lanka and Mozambique often run out of money. At that point, most governments—especially authoritarian ones—prefer the quick fix of borrowing against their country's future from the IMF.

As for the World Bank, it states that its job is to provide credit to developing countries to "reduce poverty, increase shared prosperity, and promote sustainable development."[38] The Bank itself is split up into five parts, ranging from the International Bank for Reconstruction and Development (IBRD), which focuses on more traditional "hard" loans to the larger developing countries (think Brazil or India), to the International Development Association (IDA), which focuses on "soft" interest-free loans with long grace periods for the poorest countries. There's also the International Finance Corporation (IFC), which allows Bank creditors to invest in private projects (especially in oil and mining), and the Multilateral Investment Guarantee Agency (MIGA), which provides insurance to companies operating in unstable environments.[39]

The World Bank group makes money in part through the Cantillon effect: By borrowing on favorable terms from its creditors and private market participants who have more direct access to cheaper capital, they then loan out those funds at higher terms to poor countries who lack that access. The IFC, for example, makes more than $1 billion per year from projects in more than a hundred countries.

World Bank loans traditionally are project- or sector-specific, and they have focused on facilitating the raw export of commodities (for example: financing the roads, tunnels, dams, and ports needed to get minerals out of the ground and into international markets) and on transforming traditional consumption agriculture into industrial agriculture or aquaculture so that countries could export more food and goods to the West.[40]

World Bank and IMF member states do not have voting power based on their population. Rather, influence was crafted seven decades ago to favor the United States, Europe, and Japan over the rest of the world. That dominance has only weakened mildly in recent years.

Today, the United States still owns far and away the largest vote share, at 15.6% of the World Bank[41] and 16.5% of the IMF,[42] enough to single-handedly veto any major decision, which requires 85% of votes at either institution. Japan owns 7.35% of the votes at the World Bank and 6.14% at the IMF; Germany, 4.21% and 5.31%; France and the United Kingdom, 3.87% and 4.03% each; and Italy, 2.49% and 3.02%.

By contrast, India with its 1.4 billion people, only has 3.04% of the World Bank's vote and just 2.63% at the IMF. less power than its former colonial master despite having a population twenty times bigger. China's 1.4 billion people get 5.7% at the World Bank and 6.08% at the IMF, roughly the same share as the Netherlands plus Canada and Australia. Brazil and Nigeria, the largest countries in Latin America and Africa, have about the same amount of sway as Italy, a former imperial power in full decline.

Tiny Switzerland with just 8.6 million people has 1.47% of votes at the World Bank, and 1.17% of votes at the IMF, roughly the same share as Pakistan, Indonesia, Bangladesh, and Ethiopia combined, despite having *ninety times* fewer people.

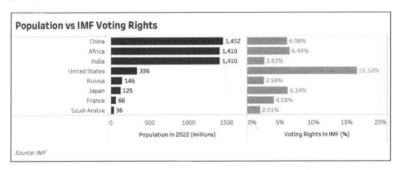

Population versus IMF voting rights.

These voting shares are supposed to approximate each country's share of the world economy, but their imperial-era structure helps color how decisions are made. Sixty-five years after decolonization, the industrial powers led by the United States continue to have more or less total control over global trade and lending, while the poorest countries have, in effect, no voice at all.

The G-5 (the United States, Japan, Germany, the United Kingdom, and France) dominate the IMF executive board, even though they make up a relatively small percent of the world's population. The G-10, plus Ireland, Australia, and Korea, make up more than 50% of the votes, meaning that, with a little pressure on its allies, the United States can make determinations even on specific loan decisions, which require a majority.[43]

To complement the IMF's trillion-dollar lending power,[44] the World Bank group claims more than $350 billion in outstanding loans across more than 150 countries.[45] This credit has spiked over the past two years, as the sister organizations have lent hundreds of billions of dollars to governments who locked down their economies in response to the COVID-19 pandemic.[46]

Over the past few months, the World Bank[47] and IMF[48] began orchestrating billion-dollar deals to "save" governments endangered by the U.S. Federal Reserve's aggressive interest rate hikes. These clients are often human rights violators, who borrow without permission from their citizens, who will ultimately be the ones responsible for paying back principal plus interest on the loans. The IMF is currently bailing out Egyptian dictator Abdel Fattah el-Sisi, who was responsible for the largest massacre of protestors since Tiananmen Square[49]—for example, with $3 billion.[50] Meanwhile, the World Bank was, during the past year, disbursing a $300 million loan[51] to an Ethiopian government that was committing war crimes in Tigray.[52]

The cumulative effect of the World Bank and IMF policies is much larger than the paper amount of their loans, as their lending drives bilateral assistance. It is estimated that "every dollar provided to the Third World by the IMF unlocks a further four to seven dollars of new loans and refinancing from commercial banks and rich-country governments." [53] Similarly, if the World Bank and IMF refuse to lend to a particular country, the rest of the world typically follows suit.

It is hard to overstate the vast impact the World Bank and IMF have had across developing nations, especially in their formative decades after World War II. By 1990 and the end of the Cold War, [54] the IMF had extended credit to forty-one countries in Africa, twenty-eight countries in Latin America, twenty countries in Asia, eight countries in the Middle East, and five countries in Europe, affecting 3 billion people, or what was then two-thirds of the global population. [55] The World Bank has extended loans to more than 160 countries. [56]

They remain the most important international financial institutions on the planet.

III. STRUCTURAL ADJUSTMENT

"Adjustment is an ever-new and never-ending task."

—Otmar Emminger,
Former IMF Director and creator of the SDR

In early 2023, financial headlines are filled with stories about IMF visits to countries like Sri Lanka[57] and Ghana.[58] The outcome is that the IMF loans billions of dollars to countries in crisis in exchange for what is known as structural adjustment.

In a structural adjustment loan, borrowers not only have to pay back principal plus interest: They also have to agree to change their economies according to World Bank and IMF demands.[59] These requirements almost always stipulate that clients maximize exports at the expense of domestic consumption.

During research for this book, the author learned much from the work of the development scholar Cheryl Payer, who wrote landmark books and papers on the influence of the World Bank and IMF in the 1970s, 1980s, and 1990s.[60] This author may disagree with Payer's "solutions"—which, like those of most critics of the World Bank and IMF, tend to be socialist—but many observations she makes about the global economy hold true regardless of ideology.

"It is an explicit and basic aim of IMF programs," she wrote, "to discourage local consumption in order to free resources for export."[61]

This point cannot be stressed enough.

The official narrative is that the World Bank and IMF were designed to "foster sustainable economic growth, promote higher standards of living, and reduce poverty."[62] But the roads and dams the World Bank builds are not designed to help improve transport and electricity for locals, but rather to make it easy for multinational corporations to extract wealth. The bailouts the IMF provides aren't to "save" a country from bankruptcy—which would probably be the best thing for it in many cases—but rather to allow it to pay its debt with even more debt, so that the original loan doesn't turn into a hole on a Western bank's balance sheet.

In her books on the World Bank and IMF, Payer describes how the institutions claim that their loan conditionality enables borrowing countries "to achieve a healthier balance of trade and payments." But the real purpose, she says, is "to bribe the governments to prevent them from making the economic changes which would make them more independent and self-supporting." When countries pay back their structural adjustment loans, debt service is prioritized, and domestic spending is to be "adjusted" downwards.

The scale of structural adjustment is astonishing. Between 1981 and 2004, 123 countries, making up 82% of the world's population, underwent structural adjustment as a result of borrowing from the World Bank or the IMF.[63]

These loans were often allocated through a mechanism called the "stand-by agreement," a line of credit that released funds only as the borrowing government claimed to achieve certain objectives.[64] From Jakarta to Lagos to Buenos Aires, IMF staff would fly in (always first or business class) to meet undemocratic rulers and offer them millions or billions of dollars in exchange for following their economic playbook.

Typical IMF demands would include:[65]

1. Currency devaluation

2. Abolition or reduction of foreign exchange and import controls

3. Shrinking of domestic bank credit

4. Higher interest rates

5. Increased taxes

6. An end to consumer subsidies on food and energy

7. Wage ceilings

8. Restrictions on government spending, especially in healthcare and education

9. Favorable legal conditions and incentives for multinational corporations

10. Selling off state enterprises and claims on natural resources at fire sale prices

The World Bank had its own playbook, too. Payer gives examples:[66]

1. The opening up of previously remote regions through transportation and telecommunications investments

2. Aiding multinational corporations in the mining sector

3. Insisting on production for export

4. Pressuring borrowers to improve legal privileges for the tax liabilities of foreign investment

5. Opposing minimum wage laws and trade union activity

6. Ending protections for locally owned businesses

7. Financing projects that appropriate land, water, and forests from poor people and hand them to multinational corporations

8. Shrinking manufacturing and food production at the expense of the export of natural resources and raw goods

Third World governments have historically been forced to agree to a mix of these policies—sometimes known as the "Washington Consensus"—in order to trigger the ongoing release of World Bank and IMF loans.[67]

The former colonial powers tend to focus their "development" lending on former colonies or areas of influence: France in West Africa, Japan in Indonesia, Britain in East Africa and South Asia, and the United States in Latin America. A notable example is the Communauté Financière Africaine (African Financial Community, or CFA) zone, where 180 million people in fifteen African countries are still forced to use a French colonial currency.[68] At the suggestion of the IMF, in 1994, France devalued the CFA by 50%,[69] devastating the savings and purchasing power of tens of millions of people living in countries ranging from Senegal to Ivory Coast to Gabon, all to make raw goods exports more competitive.[70]

The outcome of World Bank and IMF policies on the Third World has been remarkably similar to what was experienced under traditional imperialism: wage deflation, a loss of autonomy, and agricultural dependency. The big difference is that, in the new system, the sword and the gun have been replaced by weaponized debt.

Over the last thirty years, structural adjustment has intensified with regard to the average number of conditions in loans extended by the World Bank and IMF. Before 1980, the World Bank did not generally make structural adjustment loans, most everything was project- or sector-specific. But since then, "spend this however you want" bailout loans with economic quid pro quos have become a growing part of World Bank policy. For the IMF, they are its lifeblood.

For example, when the IMF bailed out South Korea and Indonesia with $57 billion and $43 billion packages during the 1997 Asian Financial Crisis, it imposed heavy conditionality.[71] Borrowers had to sign agreements that "looked more like Christmas trees than contracts, with anywhere from 50 to 80 detailed conditions covering everything from the deregulation of garlic monopolies to taxes on cattle feed and new environmental laws."[72]

A 2014 analysis showed that the IMF had attached, on average, twenty conditions to each loan it gave out in the previous two years, a historic increase. [73] Countries like Jamaica, Greece, and Cyprus have borrowed in recent years with an average of thirty-five conditions each.[74] It is worth noting that World Bank and IMF conditions have never included protections on free speech or human rights, or restrictions on military spending or police violence.

An added twist of World Bank and IMF policy is what is known as the "double loan": Money is lent to build, for example, a hydroelectric dam, but most if not all of the money gets paid to Western companies. So, the Third World taxpayer is saddled with principal and interest, and the North gets paid back double.

The context for the double loan is that dominant states extend credit through the World Bank and IMF to former colonies, where local rulers often spend the new cash directly back to multinational companies who profit from advising, construction, or import services. The ensuing and required currency devaluation, wage controls, and bank credit tightening, imposed by World Bank and IMF structural adjustments, disadvantage local entrepreneurs who are stuck in a collapsing and isolated fiat system, and benefit multinationals who are dollar, euro, or yen native.

Another key source for this author has been the masterful book, *The Lords of Poverty*, by historian Graham Hancock, written to reflect on the first five decades of World Bank and IMF policy and foreign assistance in general.

"The World Bank," Hancock writes, "is the first to admit that out of every $10 that it receives, around $7 are in fact spent on goods and services from the rich industrialized countries."

In the 1980s, when World Bank funding was expanding rapidly around the world, he noted that "for every US tax dollar contributed, 82 cents are immediately returned to American businesses in the form of purchase orders."[75] This dynamic applies not just to loans but also to aid. For example, when the United States or Germany sends a rescue plane to a country in crisis, the cost of transport, food, medicine, and staff salaries are added to what is known as ODA, or "official development assistance." On the books, it looks like aid and assistance. But most of the money is paid right back to Western companies and not invested locally.

Reflecting on the Third World Debt Crisis of the 1980s, Hancock noted that "70 cents out of every dollar of American assistance never actually left the United States." The United Kingdom, for its part, spent a whopping 80% of its aid during that time directly on British goods and services.

"One year," Hancock writes, "British tax-payers provided multilateral aid agencies with 495 million pounds; in the same year, however, British firms received contracts worth 616 million pounds." Hancock said that multilateral agencies could be "relied upon to purchase British goods and services with a value equivalent to 120% of Britain's total multilateral contribution."

One starts to see how the "aid and assistance" we tend to think of as charitable is really quite the opposite.

And as Hancock points out, foreign aid budgets always increase no matter the outcome. Just as progress is evidence that the aid is working, a "lack of progress is evidence that the dosage has been insufficient and must be increased."

Some development advocates, he writes, "argue that it would be inexpedient to deny aid to the speedy (those who advance); others, that it would be cruel to deny it to the needy (those who stagnate). Aid is thus like champagne: in success you deserve it, in failure you need it."

IV. THE DEBT TRAP

"The concept of the Third World or the South and the policy of official aid are inseparable. They are two sides of the same coin. The Third World is the creation of the foreign aid: without foreign aid there is no Third World."

—*Péter Tamás Bauer*

According to the World Bank, its objective is "to help raise living standards in developing countries by channeling financial resources from developed countries to the developing world."

But what if the reality is the opposite?

At first, beginning in the 1960s, there was an enormous flow of resources from rich countries to poor ones. This was ostensibly done to help them develop. Cheryl Payer writes that it was long considered "natural" for capital to "flow in one direction only from the developed industrial economies to the Third World."

But, as she reminds us, "at some point the borrower has to pay more to his creditor than he has received from the creditor [...] over the life of the loan this excess is much higher than the amount that was originally borrowed."

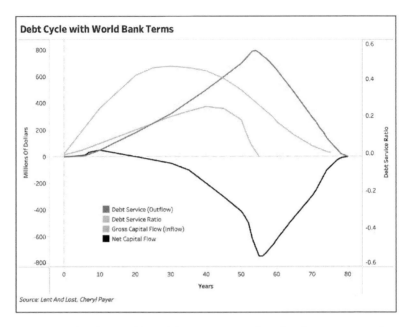

The life cycle of a World Bank loan: positive, then deeply negative cash flows for the borrower country.

In global economics, this point happened in 1982, when the flow of resources *permanently reversed.* Ever since, there has been an annual net flow of funds from poor countries to rich ones. This began as an average of $30 billion per year flowing from South to North in the mid-to-late 1980s, and is today in the range of trillions of dollars per year.[76] Between 1970 and 2007—from the end of the gold standard to the Great Financial Crisis—the total debt service paid by poor countries to rich ones was $7.15 trillion.[77]

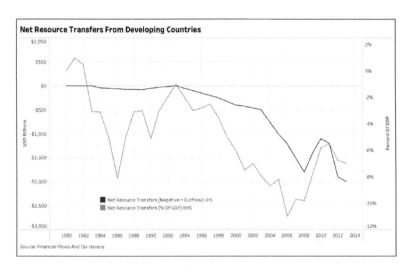

*Net resource transfers from developing countries,increasingly negative
since 1982.*

To give an example of what this might look like in a given
year, in 2012, developing countries received $1.3 trillion,
including all income, aid, and investment.[78] But that same
year, more than $3.3 trillion flowed out. In other words,
according to anthropologist Jason Hickel, "developing
countries sent $2 trillion more to the rest of the world than
they received."[79]

When all the flows were added up from 1960 to 2017, a
grim truth emerged: $62 trillion was drained out of the
developing world, the equivalent of 620 Marshall Plans in
today's dollars.[80]

The IMF and World Bank were supposed to fix balance
of payments issues and help poor countries grow stronger and
more sustainable. The evidence has been the direct opposite.

"For every $1 of aid that developing countries receive," Hickel writes, "they lose $24 in net outflows." Instead of ending exploitation and unequal exchange, studies show that structural adjustment policies grew them in a massive way.[81]

Since 1970, the external public debt of developing countries has increased from $46 billion to $8.7 trillion.[82] In the past fifty years, countries like India and the Philippines and the Congo now owe their former colonial masters *189 times* the amount they owed in 1970. They have paid $4.2 trillion on *interest payments alone* since 1980.[83]

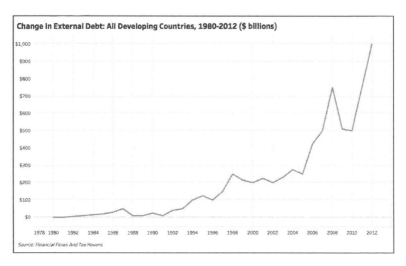

The exponential rise in developing country debt.

Today, the debt trap for developing countries is deeper than ever. Nigeria, for example, was forced to allocate 80% of its national revenue in 2022 to servicing debt.[84] The country has shaped its economy to try and pay back debt instead of investing in its future.

In Payer's 1974 book, *The Debt Trap*, she used economic flow data to show how the IMF ensnared poor countries by encouraging them to borrow more than they could possibly pay back. But even she would be shocked at the size of today's debt trap.

Her observation that "the average citizen of the US or Europe may not be aware of this enormous drain in capital from parts of the world they think of as being pitifully poor" still rings true today. To this author's own shame, he did not know about the true nature of the global flow of funds and simply assumed that rich countries subsidized poor ones before embarking on the research for this project. The end result is a literal Ponzi scheme, where by the 1970s, Third World debt was so big that it was only possible to service with new debt. It has been the same ever since.

Many critics of the World Bank and IMF assume that these institutions are working with their heart in the right place, and when they do fail, it is because of mistakes, waste, or mismanagement.

It is the thesis of this book that this is not true, and that the foundational goals of the IMF and World Bank are not to fix poverty but rather to enrich creditor nations at the expense of poor ones.

This author is simply not willing to believe that a permanent flow of funds from poor countries to rich ones since 1982 is a "mistake." The reader may dispute that the arrangement is intentional, and rather may believe it is an unconscious structural outcome. The difference hardly matters to the billions of people the World Bank and IMF have impoverished.

V. REPLACING THE COLONIAL RESOURCE DRAIN

"I am so tired of waiting. Aren't you, for the world to become good and beautiful and kind? Let us take a knife and cut the world in two—and see what worms are eating at the rind."

—*Langston Hughes*

By the end of the 1950s, Europe and Japan had largely recovered from war and resumed significant industrial growth, while Third World countries ran out of funds. Despite having healthy balance sheets in the 1940s and early 1950s, poor, raw material–exporting countries ran into balance-of-payments issues as the value of their commodities tanked in the wake of the Korean War.[85] This is when the debt trap began, and when the World Bank and IMF started the floodgates of what would end up becoming trillions of dollars of lending.

This era also marked the official end of colonialism, as European empires drew back from their imperial possessions. The established assumption in international development is that the economic success of nations is due "primarily to their internal, domestic conditions.[86] High-income countries have achieved economic success," the theory goes, "because of

good governance, strong institutions, and free markets.
Lower-income countries have failed to develop because they
lack these things, or because they suffer from corruption, red
tape, and inefficiency."

This is certainly true. But another major reason why rich
countries are rich and poor countries are poor is that the
former looted the latter for hundreds of years during the
colonial period.

"Britain's industrial revolution," Jason Hickel writes,
"depended in large part on cotton, which was grown on land
forcibly appropriated from Indigenous Americans, with labor
appropriated from enslaved Africans. Other crucial inputs
required by British manufacturers—hemp, timber, iron,
grain—were produced using forced labor on serf estates in
Russia and Eastern Europe. Meanwhile, British extraction
from India and other colonies funded more than half the
country's domestic budget, paying for roads, public buildings,
the welfare state—all the markets of modern development—
while enabling the purchase of material inputs necessary for
industrialization."[87]

The theft dynamic was described by Utsa and Prabhat
Patnaik in their book, *Capital and Imperialism*: Colonial
powers, like the British empire, would use violence to extract
raw materials from weak countries, creating a "colonial drain"
of capital that boosted and subsidized life in London, Paris,
and Berlin. Industrial nations would transform these raw
materials into manufactured goods, and sell them back to
weaker nations, profiting massively while also crowding out

local production. And—critically—they would keep inflation at home down by suppressing wages in the colonial territories. Either through outright slavery or through paying well below the global market rate.

As the colonial system began to falter, the Western financial world faced a crisis. The Patnaiks argue that the Great Depression was a result, not simply of changes in Western monetary policy, but also of the colonial drain slowing down. The reasoning is simple: Rich countries had built a conveyor belt of resources flowing from poor countries, and when the belt broke, so did everything else. Between the 1920s and 1960s, political colonialism became virtually extinct. Britain, the United States, Germany, France, Japan, the Netherlands, Belgium, and other empires were forced to give up control over more than half of the world's territory and resources.

As the Patnaiks write, imperialism is "an arrangement for imposing income deflation on the Third World population in order to get their primary commodities without running into the problem of increasing supply price."

Post-1960, this became the new function for the World Bank and IMF: recreating the colonial drain from poor countries to rich countries that was once maintained by straightforward imperialism.

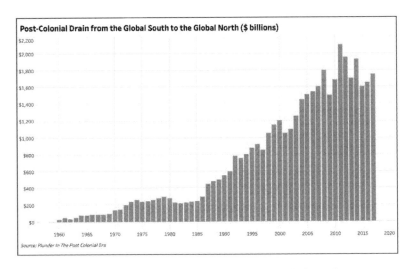

Post-colonial drain from the Global South to the Global North.

Officials in the United States, Europe, and Japan wanted to achieve "internal equilibrium"—in other words, full employment. But they realized they could not do this via subsidy inside an isolated system, or else inflation would run rampant. To achieve their goal, Western governments would require external input from poorer countries. The extra surplus value extracted by the core from workers in the periphery is known as "imperialist rent."[88] If industrial countries could get cheaper materials and labor, and then sell the finished goods back at a profit, they could inch closer to the technocrat dream economy. And they got their wish: As of 2019, wages paid to workers in the developing world were only 20% of the level of wages paid to workers in the developed world.[89]

As an example of how the World Bank recreated the colonial drain dynamic, Cheryl Payer gives the classic case of

1960s Mauritania in northwest Africa. A mining project called MIFERMA was signed by French occupiers before the colony became independent. The deal eventually became "just an old-fashioned enclave project: a city in a desert and a railroad leading to the ocean," as the infrastructure was solely focused on spiriting minerals away to international markets. In 1969, when the mine accounted for 30% of Mauritania's GDP and 75% of its exports, 72% of the income was sent abroad, and "practically all the income distributed locally to employees evaporated in imports." When the miners protested against the neocolonial arrangement, security forces savagely put them down.

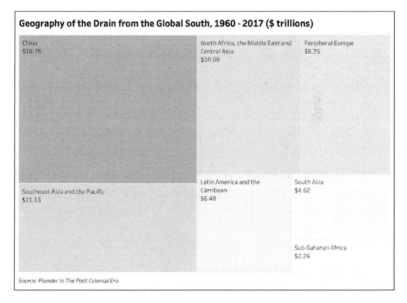

Geography of the drain from the Global South from 1960 to 2017.

MIFERMA is a stereotypical example of the kind of "development" that would be imposed on the Third World everywhere from the Dominican Republic to Madagascar to Cambodia. And all of these projects rapidly expanded in the 1970s, thanks to the petrodollar system.

Post-1973, Arab Organization of the Petroleum Exporting Countries (OPEC), with enormous surpluses from skyrocketing oil prices, sank their profits into deposits and treasuries in Western banks, which needed a place to lend out their growing resources. Military dictators across Latin America, Africa, and Asia made great targets: They had high time preferences and were happy to borrow against future generations.

Helping expedite loan growth was the "IMF put": Private banks started to believe (correctly) that the IMF would bail out countries if they defaulted, protecting their investments. Moreover, interest rates in the mid-1970s were often in negative real territory, further encouraging borrowers. This— combined with World Bank President Robert McNamara's insistence that assistance expand dramatically—resulted in a debt frenzy. U.S. banks, for example, increased their Third World loan portfolio by 300% to $450 billion between 1978 and 1982.

The problem was that these loans were in large part floating interest rate agreements, and a few years later, those rates exploded as the U.S. Federal Reserve raised the global cost of capital close to 20%. The growing debt burden— combined with the 1979 oil price shock and the ensuing global collapse in the price of commodities that power the value of developing country exports—paved the way for the Third World Debt Crisis.[90] To make matters worse, very little of the money borrowed by governments during the debt frenzy was actually invested in the average citizen.

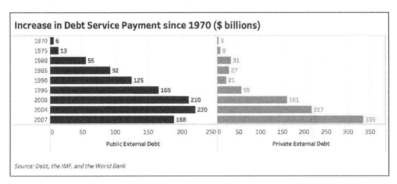

Third World debt service over time.

In their aptly named book, *Debt Squads*, investigative journalists Sue Branford and Bernardo Kucinski explain that, between 1976 and 1981, Latin governments (of which eighteen of twenty-one were dictatorships) borrowed $272.9 billion. Out of that, 91.6% was spent on debt servicing, capital flight, and building up regime reserves. Only 8.4% was used on domestic investment, and even out of that, much was wasted.

Brazilian civil society advocate Carlos Ayuda vividly described the effect of the petrodollar-fueled drain on his own country:

"The military dictatorship used the loans to invest in huge infrastructure projects—particularly energy projects […] the idea behind creating an enormous hydroelectric dam and plant in the middle of the Amazon, for example, was to produce aluminum for export to the North [...] the government took out huge loans and invested billions of dollars in building the Tucuruí dam in the late 1970s, destroying native forests and removing massive numbers of native peoples and poor rural people that had lived there for generations. The government would have razed the forests, but the deadlines were so short they used Agent Orange to defoliate the region and then submerged the leafless tree trunks underwater [...] the hydroelectric plant's energy [was then] sold at $13–20 per megawatt when the actual price of production was $48. So the taxpayers provided subsidies, financing cheap energy for transnational corporations to sell our aluminum in the international market."[91]

In other words, the Brazilian people paid foreign creditors for the service of destroying their environment, displacing the masses, and selling their resources.

In 2023, the drain from low- and middle-income countries to rich ones is staggering. In 2015, it totaled 10.1 billion tons of raw materials and 182 million person-years of labor: 50% of all goods and 28% of all labor used that year by high-income countries. [92] Now imagine life in the West without half of the available resources or nearly one-third of the available labor. Or if the West had to pay much higher prices for half of the resources it consumes or for nearly one-third of the labor it relies on. Then you start to understand how poor countries continue to subsidize the way of life of people in rich ones.

VI. A DANCE WITH DICTATORS

"He may be a son of a bitch, but he's our son of a bitch."

—*Franklin Delano Roosevelt*

Of course, it takes two sides to finalize a loan from the World Bank or IMF. The problem is that the borrower is typically an unelected or unaccountable leader, who makes the decision without consulting with, and without a popular mandate, from their citizens.

As Cheryl Payer writes in *The Debt Trap*, "IMF programs are politically unpopular, for the very good concrete reasons that they hurt local business and depress the real income of the electorate. A government which attempts to carry out the conditions in its Letter of Intent to the IMF is likely to find itself voted out of office."

Hence, the IMF prefers to work with undemocratic clients who can more easily dismiss troublesome judges and put down street protests. According to Payer, the military coups in Brazil in 1964, Turkey in 1960, Indonesia in 1966, Argentina in 1966, and the Philippines in 1972 were examples of IMF-opposed leaders being forcibly replaced by IMF-friendly ones. Even if the IMF wasn't directly involved in the coup, in each of these cases, it arrived enthusiastically a few days, weeks, or months later to help the new regime implement structural adjustment.

The World Bank and IMF share a willingness to support abusive governments. Perhaps surprisingly, it was the World Bank that started the tradition. According to development researcher Kevin Danaher, "the Bank's sad record of supporting military regimes and governments that openly violated human rights began on August 7, 1947, with a $195 million reconstruction loan to the Netherlands. Seventeen days before the Bank approved the loan, the Netherlands had unleashed a war against anti-colonialist nationalist in its huge overseas empire in the East Indies, which had already declared its independence as the Republic of Indonesia."

"The Dutch," Danaher writes, "sent 145,000 troops (from a nation with only 10 million inhabitants at the time, economically struggling at 90% of 1939 production) and launched a total economic blockade of nationalist-held areas, causing considerable hunger and health problems among Indonesia's 70 million inhabitants."

In its first few decades, the World Bank funded many such colonial schemes, including $28 million for apartheid Rhodesia in 1952, as well as loans to Australia, the United Kingdom, and Belgium to "develop" colonial possessions in Papua New Guinea, Kenya, and the Belgian Congo.[93]

In 1966, Danaher writes that the World Bank directly defied the United Nations, "continuing to lend money to South Africa and Portugal despite resolutions of the General

Assembly calling on all UN-affiliated agencies to cease financial support for both countries."

Danaher says, "Portugal's colonial domination of Angola and Mozambique and South Africa's apartheid were flagrant violations of the UN charter. But the World Bank argued that Article IV, Section 10, of its Charter which prohibits interference in the political affairs of any member, legally obliged it to disregard the UN resolutions. As a result the World Bank approved loans of $10 million to Portugal and $20 million to South Africa after the UN resolution was passed."

Sometimes, the World Bank's preference for tyranny was stark: It cut off lending to the democratically elected Allende government in Chile in the early 1970s, but shortly after began to lend huge quantities of cash to Ceausescu's Romania, one of the world's worst police states. This is also an example of how the World Bank and IMF, contrary to popular belief, didn't simply lend along Cold War ideological lines: For every right-wing Augusto Pinochet Ugarte or Jorge Rafael Videla client, there was a left-wing Josip Broz Tito or Julius Nyerere.

In 1979, Danaher notes, fifteen of the world's most repressive governments would receive a full third of all World Bank loans. This even after the U.S. Congress and the Carter administration had stopped aid to four of the fifteen— Argentina, Chile, Uruguay, and Ethiopia—for "flagrant human rights violations." Just a few years later, in El Salvador, the IMF made a $43 million loan to the military

dictatorship,[94] just a few months after its forces committed the largest massacre in Cold War–era Latin America by annihilating the village of El Mozote.[95]

There were several books written about the World Bank and the IMF in 1994, timed as fifty-year retrospectives on the Bretton Woods institutions. *Perpetuating Poverty* by Ian Vàsquez and Doug Bandow is one of those studies, and it's a particularly valuable one as it provides a Libertarian analysis. Most critical studies of the World Bank and IMF are from the left, but the Cato Institute's Vásquez and Bandow saw many of the same problems.

"The Fund underwrites any government," they write, "however venal and brutal […] China owed the Fund $600 million as of the end of 1989; in January 1990, just a few months after the blood had dried in Beijing's Tiananmen Square, the IMF held a seminar on monetary policy in the city."

Vásquez and Bandow mention other tyrannical clients ranging from military Burma, to Pinochet's Chile, Laos, , Syria, Vietnam, and Nicaragua under Anastasio Somoza Debayle and the Sandinistas.

"The IMF," they say, "has rarely met a dictatorship that it did not like."

Vásquez and Bandow detail the World Bank's relationship with the Marxist–Leninist Mengistu Haile Mariam regime in Ethiopia, where it provided for as much as 16% of the government's annual budget while it had one of the worst human rights records in the world. The World Bank's credit arrived just as Mengistu's forces were "herding people into concentration camps and collective farms." They also point out how the World Bank gave the Sudanese regime $16 million while it was driving 750,000 refugees out of Khartoum into the desert, and how it gave hundreds of millions of dollars to Iran—a brutal theocratic dictatorship— and Mozambique, whose security forces were infamous for torture, rape, and summary executions.

In his 2011 book, *Defeating Dictators*, the celebrated Ghanaian development economist George Ayittey detailed a long list of "aid-receiving autocrats": Paul Biya, Idriss Déby, Lansana Conté, Paul Kagame, Yoweri Museveni, Hun Sen, Islam Karimov, Nursultan Nazarbayev, and Emomali Rahmon. He pointed out that the IMF had dispensed $75 billion to these nine tyrants alone.

In 2014, a report was released by the International Consortium of Investigative Journalists (ICIJ), alleging that the Ethiopian government had used part of a $2 billion World Bank loan to forcibly relocate 37,883 indigenous Anuak families.[96] This was 60% of the country's entire Gambela province. Soldiers "beat, raped, and killed" Anuak who refused to leave their homes. Atrocities were so bad that *South Sudan* granted refugee status to Anuaks streaming in from neighboring Ethiopia.[97] A Human Rights Watch report said that the stolen land was then "leased by the government to investors" and that the World Bank's money was "used to pay the salaries of government officials who helped carry out the evictions." The World Bank approved new funding for this

"villagization" program even after allegations of mass human
rights violations emerged.

Source: Jack E. Kightlinger

Mobutu Sese Soko and Richard Nixon at the White House in 1973.

It would be a mistake to leave Mobutu Sese Soko's Zaire
out of this study. The recipient of billions of dollars of World
Bank and IMF credit during his bloody thirty-two-year reign,
Mobutu pocketed 30% of incoming aid and assistance and let
his people starve. He complied with eleven IMF structural
adjustments: During one in 1984, 46,000 public school
teachers were fired and the national currency was devalued by
80%.[98] Mobutu called this austerity "a bitter pill which we
have no alternative but to swallow," but didn't sell any of his
fifty-one Mercedes, any of his eleven chateaus in Belgium or
France, or even his Boeing 747 or sixteenth-century Spanish
castle.

Per capita income declined in each year of his rule on average by 2.2%, leaving more than 80% of the population in absolute poverty.[99] Children routinely died before the age of five, and "swollen belly" syndrome was rampant. It is estimated that Mobutu personally stole $5 billion, and presided over another $12 billion in capital flight, which together would have been more than enough to wipe the country's $14 billion debt clean at the time of his ouster.[100] He looted and terrorized his people and could not have done it without the World Bank and IMF, which continued to bail him out even though it was clear he would never repay his debts.

All that said, the true poster boy for the World Bank and IMF's affection for dictators might be Ferdinand Marcos. In 1966, when Marcos came to power, the Philippines was the second-most prosperous country in Asia, and the country's foreign debt stood at roughly $500 million. By the time Marcos was removed in 1986, the debt stood at $28.1 billion.

As Graham Hancock writes in *Lords of Poverty*, most of these loans "had been contracted to pay for extravagant development schemes which, although irrelevant to the poor, had pandered to the enormous ego of the head of state [...] a painstaking two-year investigation established beyond serious dispute that he had personally expropriated and sent out of the Philippines more than $10 billion. Much of this money—which of course, should have been at the disposal of the Philippine state and people—had disappeared forever in Swiss bank accounts."

"$100 million," Hancock writes, "was paid for the art collection for Imelda Marcos […] her tastes were eclectic and included six Old Masters purchased from the Knoedler Gallery in New York for $5 million, a Francis Bacon canvas supplied by the Marlborough Gallery in London, and a Michelangelo, 'Madonna and Child' bought from Mario Bellini in Florence for $3.5 million."

"During the last decade of the Marcos regime," he says, "while valuable art treasuries were being hung on penthouse walls in Manhattan and Paris, the Philippines had lower nutritional standards than any other nation in Asia with the exception of war-torn Cambodia."

To contain popular unrest, Hancock writes that Marcos banned strikes and "union organizing was outlawed in all key industries and in agriculture. Thousands of Filipinos were imprisoned for opposing the dictatorship and many were tortured and killed. Meanwhile the country remained consistently listed among the top recipients of both US and World Bank development assistance."

After the Filipino people pushed Marcos out, they still had to pay an annual sum of anywhere between 40% and 50% of the entire value of their exports "just to cover the interest on the foreign debts that Marcos incurred."

One would think that after ousting Marcos, the Filipino people would not have to owe the debt he incurred on their behalf without consulting them. But that is not how it has worked in practice. In theory, this concept is called "odious debt" and was invented by the United States in 1898 when it repudiated Cuba's debt after Spanish forces were ousted from the island.[101]

American leaders determined that debts "incurred to subjugate a people or to colonize them" were not legitimate. But the World Bank and IMF have never followed this precedent during their seventy-five years of operations. Ironically, the IMF has an article on its website suggesting that Somoza, Marcos, Apartheid South Africa, Haiti's "Baby Doc," and Nigeria's Sani Abacha all borrowed billions illegitimately, and that the debt should be written off for their victims, but this remains a suggestion unfollowed.[102]

Technically and morally speaking, a large percentage of Third World debt should be considered "odious" and not owed anymore by the population should their dictator be forced out. After all, in most cases, the citizens paying back the loans didn't elect their leader and didn't choose to borrow the loans that they took out against their future.

In July 1987, the revolutionary leader Thomas Sankara gave a speech to the Organization of African Unity (OAU) in Ethiopia, where he refused to pay the colonial debt of Burkina Faso, and encouraged other African nations to join him.[103]

"We cannot pay," he said, "because we are not responsible for this debt."

Sankara famously boycotted the IMF and refused structural adjustment. Three months after his OAU speech, he was assassinated by Blaise Compaoré,[104] who would install his own twenty-seven-year military regime that would receive four structural adjustment loans from the IMF[105] and borrow dozens of times from the World Bank for various infrastructure and agriculture projects. [106] Since Sankara's death, few heads of state have been willing to take a stand to repudiate their debts.

Source: AFP / Stringer

Burkinese dictator Blaise Compaoré and IMF Managing Director Dominique Strauss-Kahn. Compaoré seized power after assassinating Thomas Sankara (who tried to refuse Western debt) and he went on to borrow billions from the World Bank and IMF.

One big exception was Iraq: After the U.S. invasion and ouster of Saddam Hussein in 2003, American authorities managed to get some of the debt incurred by Hussein to be considered "odious" and forgiven.[107] But this was a unique case, for the billions of people who suffered under colonialists or dictators, and have since been forced to pay their debts plus interest, they have not gotten this special treatment

In recent years, the IMF has even acted as a counter-revolutionary force against democratic movements. In the 1990s, the IMF was widely criticized on the left[108] and the right for helping to destabilize the former Soviet Union as it descended into economic chaos and congealed into Vladimir Putin's dictatorship.[109] In 2011, as the Arab Spring protests emerged across the Middle East, the Deauville Partnership with Arab Countries in Transition was formed and met in Paris, France.[110]

Through this mechanism, the World Bank and IMF led massive loan offers to Yemen, Tunisia, Egypt, Morocco, and Jordan—"Arab countries in Transition"—in exchange for structural adjustment.[111] As a result, Tunisia's foreign debt skyrocketed, triggering two new IMF loans, marking the first time that the country had borrowed from the IMF since 1988. The austerity measures paired with these loans forced the devaluation of the Tunisian dinar, which spiked prices.[112] National protests broke out as the government continued to follow the IMF playbook with wage freezes, new taxes, and "early retirement" in the public sector.

Twenty-nine-year-old protestor Warda Atig summed up the situation: "As long as Tunisia continues these deals with the IMF, we will continue our struggle," she said. "We believe that the IMF and the interests of people are contradictory. An escape from submission to the IMF, which has brought Tunisia to its knees and strangled the economy, is a prerequisite to bring about any real change."

VII. CREATING AGRICULTURAL DEPENDENCE

"The idea that developing countries should feed themselves is an anachronism from a bygone era. They could better ensure their food security by relying on the U.S. agricultural products, which are available in most cases at lower cost."

— *John Block*
Former U.S. Secretary of Agriculture

As a result of World Bank and IMF policy, all across Latin America, Africa, the Middle East, and South and East Asia, countries which once grew their own food now import it from rich countries. Growing one's own food is important, in retrospect, because in the post-1944 financial system, commodities are not priced with one's local fiat currency: They are priced in the dollar.

Consider the price of wheat, which ranged between $200 and $300 between 1996 and 2006. It has since skyrocketed, peaking at nearly $1,100 in 2021.[113] If your country grew its own wheat, it could weather the storm. If your country had to import wheat, your population risked starvation. This is one reason why countries like Pakistan,[114] Sri Lanka,[115] Egypt,[116] Ghana,[117] and Bangladesh[118] are all currently turning to the IMF for emergency loans.

Historically, where the World Bank did give loans, they were mostly for "modern," large-scale, mono-crop agriculture and for resource extraction: not for the development of local industry, manufacturing, or consumption farming. [119] Borrowers were encouraged to focus on raw materials exports (oil, minerals, coffee, cocoa, palm oil, tea, rubber, cotton, etc.), and then pushed to import finished goods, food stuffs, and the ingredients for modern agriculture like fertilizer, pesticides, tractors, and irrigation machinery. The result is that societies like Morocco end up importing wheat and soybean oil instead of thriving on native couscous and olive oil, "fixed" to become dependent. [120] Earnings were typically used not to benefit farmers, but to service foreign debt, purchase weapons, import luxury goods, fill Swiss bank accounts, and put down dissent. [121]

Consider some of the world's poorest countries. As of 2020, after fifty years of World Bank and IMF policy, Niger's exports were 75% uranium; [122] Mali's 72% gold; [123] Zambia's 70% copper; [124] Burundi's 69% coffee; [125] Malawi's 55% tobacco; [126] Togo's 50% cotton; [127] and on it goes. At times in past decades, these single exports supported virtually all of these countries' hard currency earnings. This is not a natural state of affairs. These items are not mined or produced for local consumption, but for French nuclear plants, Chinese electronics, German supermarkets, British cigarette makers, and American clothing companies. In other words, the energy of the labor force of these nations has been engineered towards feeding and powering other civilizations, instead of nourishing and advancing their own.

Researcher Alicia Koren, in Kevin Danaher's *50 Years Is Enough*, wrote about the typical agricultural impact of World Bank policy in Costa Rica, where the country's "structural adjustment called for earning more hard currency to pay off foreign debt; forcing farmers who traditionally grew beans, rice, and corn for domestic consumption to plant non-traditional agricultural exports such as ornamental plants, flowers, melons, strawberries, and red peppers [...] industries that exported their products were eligible for tariff and tax exemptions not available to domestic producers."

"Meanwhile," Koren wrote, "structural adjustment agreements removed support for domestic production [...] while the North pressured Southern nations to eliminate subsidies and 'barriers to trade,' Northern governments pumped billions of dollars into their own agricultural sectors, making it impossible for basic grains growers in the South to compete with the North's highly subsidized agricultural industry."

Koren extrapolated her Costa Rica analysis to make a broader point: "Structural adjustment agreements shift public spending subsidies from basic supplies, consumed mainly by the poor and middle classes, to luxury export crops produced for affluent foreigners." Third World countries were not seen as body politics but as companies that needed to increase revenues and decrease expenditures.

The testimony of a former Jamaican official is especially telling: "We told the World Bank team that farmers could hardly afford credit, and that higher rates would put them out of business. The Bank told us in response that this means 'The market is telling you that agriculture is not the way to go for Jamaica'—they are saying we should give up farming altogether."

"The World Bank and IMF," the official said, "don't have to worry about the farmers and local companies going out of business, or starvation wages or the social upheaval that will result. They simply assume that it is our job to keep our national security forces strong enough to suppress any uprising."

Developing governments are stuck: Faced with insurmountable debt, the only factor they really control in terms of increasing revenue is deflating wages. If they do this, they must provide basic food subsidies, or else they will be overthrown. And so the debt grows.

Even when developing countries try to produce their own food, they are crowded out by a centrally planned, global trade market. For example, one would think that the cheap labor in a place like West Africa would make it a better exporter of peanuts than the United States. But since Northern countries pay an estimated $1 billion in subsidies to their agriculture industries every single day, Southern countries often struggle to be competitive.[128] What's worse, fifty or sixty countries are often directed to focus on the very same crops, crowding each other out in the global marketplace. Rubber, palm oil, coffee, tea, and cotton are World Bank favorites, as the poor masses can't eat them.[129]

It is true that the Green Revolution has created more food for the planet, especially in China and East Asia.[130] But despite advances in agricultural technology, much of these new yields go to exports, and vast swathes of the world remain chronically malnourished and dependent. To this day, for example, African nations import about 85% of their food.[131] They pay more than $40 billion per year—a number estimated to reach $110 billion per year by 2025—to buy from other parts of the world what they could grow themselves.[132] World Bank and IMF policy helped transform a continent of incredible agricultural riches into one reliant on the outside world to feed its people.

Reflecting on the results of this policy of dependency, Graham Hancock challenges the widespread belief that the people of the Third World are "fundamentally helpless."

"Victims of nameless crises, disasters, and catastrophes," he writes, suffer from a perception that "they can do nothing unless we, the rich and powerful, intervene to save them from themselves." But as evidenced by the fact that our "assistance" has only made them more dependent on us, Hancock rightfully unmasks the notion that "only we can save them" as "patronizing and profoundly fallacious."

Far from playing the role of good Samaritan, the IMF does not even follow the timeless human tradition, established more than four thousand years ago by Hammurabi in ancient Babylon, of forgiving interest after natural disasters. In 1985, a devastating earthquake hit Mexico City, killing more than five thousand people and causing $5 billion of damage.[133]

IMF staff—who claim to be saviors, helping to end poverty and save countries in crisis—arrived a few days later, demanding to be repaid.

VIII. YOU CAN'T EAT COTTON

"Development prefers crops that can't be eaten so the loans can be collected."

—Cheryl Payer

The Togolese democracy advocate Farida Nabourema's own personal and family experience tragically matches the big picture of the World Bank and IMF laid out thus far.

The way she puts it, after the 1970s oil boom, loans were poured into developing nations like Togo, whose unaccountable rulers didn't think twice about how they would repay the debt. Much of the money went into giant infrastructure projects that didn't help the majority of the people. Much was embezzled and spent on pharaonic estates. Most of these countries, she says, were ruled by single party-states or families. Once interest rates started to hike, these governments could no longer pay their debts: The IMF started "taking over" by imposing austerity measures.

"These were new states that were very fragile," Nabourema says in an interview for this book. "They needed to invest strongly in social infrastructure, just as the European states were allowed to do after World War II. But instead, we went from free healthcare and education one day, to situations the next where it became too costly for the average person to get even basic medicine."

Regardless of what one thinks about state-subsidized medicine and schooling, eliminating it overnight was traumatic for poor countries. World Bank and IMF officials, of course, have their own private healthcare solutions for their visits and their own private schools for their children whenever they have to live "in the field."

Because of the forced cuts in public spending, Nabourema says, the state hospitals in Togo remain to this day in "complete decay." Unlike the state-run, taxpayer-financed public hospitals in the capitals of former colonial powers in London and Paris, things are so bad in Togo's capital Lomé that even water has to be prescribed.

"There was also," Nabourema said, "reckless privatization of our public companies." She explained how her father used to work at the Togolese steel agency. During privatization, the company was sold off to foreign actors for less than half of what the state built it for.

"It was basically a garage sale," she said.

Nabourema says that a free-market system and liberal reforms work well when all participants are on an equal playing field. But that is not the case in Togo, which is forced to play by different rules. No matter how much it opens up, it can't change the strict policies of the United States and Europe, who aggressively subsidize their own industries and agriculture. Nabourema mentions how a subsidized influx of cheap used clothes from America, for example, ruined Togo's local textile industry.

"These clothes from the West," she said, "put entrepreneurs out of business and littered our beaches."

The most horrible aspect, she said, is that the farmers—who made up 60% of the population in Togo in the 1980s—had their livelihoods turned upside down. The dictatorship needed hard currency to pay its debts and could only do this by selling exports, so they began a massive campaign to sell cash crops. With the World Bank's help, the regime invested heavily in cotton, so much so that it now dominates 50% of the country's exports, destroying national food security.

In the formative years for countries like Togo, the World Bank was the "largest single lender for agriculture." Its strategy for fighting poverty was agricultural modernization: "massive transfers of capital, in the form of fertilizers, pesticides, earth-moving equipment, and expensive foreign consultants." [134]

Nabourema's father was the one who revealed to her how imported fertilizers and tractors were diverted away from farmers growing consumption food to farmers growing cash crops like cotton, coffee, cocoa, and cashews. If someone was growing corn, sorghum, or millet—the basic food stuffs of the population—they didn't get access.

"You can't eat cotton," Nabourema reminds us.

Over time, the political elite in countries like Togo and Benin (where the dictator was literally a cotton mogul[135]) became the buyer of all the cash crops from all of the farms. They'd have a monopoly on purchases, Nabourema says, and would buy the crops for prices so low that the peasants would barely make any money. This entire system—called *sotoco* in Togo—was based on funding provided by the World Bank.

When farmers would protest, she said, they would get beaten or their farms would get burned to rubble. They could have just grown normal food and fed their families, like they had done for generations. But now they could not even afford the land: The political elite has been acquiring land at an outrageous rate, often through illegal means, jacking up the price.

As an example, Nabourema explains how the Togolese regime might seize two thousand acres of land: Unlike in a liberal democracy (like the one in France, which has built its civilization off the backs of countries like Togo), the judicial system is owned by the government, so there is no way to push back. So farmers, who used to be self-sovereign, are now forced to work as laborers on someone else's land to provide cotton to rich countries far away. The most tragic irony, Nabourema says, is that cotton is overwhelmingly grown in the north of Togo, in the poorest part of the country.

"But when you go there," she says, "you see it has made no one rich."

Women bear the brunt of structural adjustment. The misogyny of the policy is "quite clear in Africa, where women are the major farmers and providers of fuel, wood, and water," Kevin Danaher writes. And yet, a recent retrospective says, "the World Bank prefers to blame them for having too many children rather than reexamining its own policies."

As Cheryl Payer writes, for many of the world's poor, they are poor "not because they have been left behind or ignored by their country's progress, but because they are the victims of modernisation. Most have been crowded off the good farmland, or deprived of land altogether, by rich elites and local or foreign agribusiness. Their destitution has not 'ruled them out' of the development process; the development process has been the cause of their destitution."

"Yet the Bank," Payer says, "is still determined to transform the agricultural practices of small farmers. Bank policy statements make it clear that the real aim is integration of peasant land into the commercial sector through the production of a 'marketable surplus' of cash crops."

Payer observed how, in the 1970s and 1980s, many small plotters still grew the bulk of their own food needs, and were not "dependent on the market for the near-totality of their sustenance, as 'modern' people were." These people, however, were the target of the World Bank's policies, which transformed them into surplus producers, and "often enforced this transformation with authoritarian methods."

In a testimony in front of U.S. Congress in the 1990s, George Ayittey remarked that "if Africa were able to feed itself, it could save nearly $15 billion it wastes on food imports. This figure may be compared with the $17 billion Africa received in foreign aid from all sources in 1997."

In other words, if Africa grew its own food, it wouldn't need foreign aid. But if that were to happen, then poor countries wouldn't be buying billions of dollars of food per year from rich countries, whose economies would shrink as a result. So the West strongly resists any change.

IX. THE DEVELOPMENT SET

Excuse me, friends, I must catch my jet
I'm off to join the Development Set
My bags are packed, and I've had all my shots
I have traveler's checks and pills for the trots!
The Development Set is bright and noble
Our thoughts are deep and our vision global
Although we move with the better classes
Our thoughts are always with the masses
In Sheraton Hotels in scattered nations
We damn multinational corporations
Injustice seems easy to protest
In such seething hotbeds of social rest.
We discuss malnutrition over steaks
And plan hunger talks during coffee breaks.
Whether Asian floods or African drought
We face each issue with open mouth.

And so begins "The Development Set,"[136] a 1976 poem by Ross Coggins that hits at the heart of the paternalistic and unaccountable nature of the World Bank and the IMF.

The World Bank pays high, tax-free salaries, with very generous benefits. IMF staff are paid even better, and traditionally, were flown first or business class (depending on the distance), never economy. They stayed in five-star hotels, and even had a perk to get free upgrades onto the supersonic Concorde. Their salaries, unlike wages made by people living under structural adjustment, were not capped and always rose faster than the inflation rate.

Until the mid-1990s the janitors cleaning the World Bank headquarters in Washington—mostly immigrants who fled from countries that the Bank and IMF had "adjusted"—were not even allowed to unionize. In contrast, Christine Lagarde's tax-free salary as head of the IMF was $467,940, plus an additional $83,760 allowance.[137] Of course, during her term from 2011 to 2019, she oversaw a variety of structural adjustments on poor countries, where taxes on the most vulnerable were almost always raised.

Graham Hancock notes that redundancy payments at the World Bank in the 1980s "averaged a quarter of a million dollars per person." When seven hundred executives lost their jobs in 1987, the money spent on their golden parachutes—$175 million—would have been enough, he notes, "to pay for a complete elementary school education for 63,000 children from poor families in Latin America or Africa."

According to former World Bank head James Wolfensohn, from 1995 to 2005 there were more than 63,000 World Bank projects in developing countries: the costs of "feasibility studies" and travel and lodging for experts from industrialized countries alone absorbed as much as 25% of the total aid.

Fifty years after the creation of the Bank and IMF, "90% of the $12 billion per year in technical assistance was still spent on foreign expertise." That year, in 1994, George Ayittey noted that 80,000 World Bank consultants worked on Africa alone, but that "less than .01%" were Africans.[138]

Hancock writes that "the World Bank, which puts more money into more schemes in more developing countries than any other institution, claims that 'it seeks to meet the needs of the poorest people;' but at no stage in what it refers to as the 'project cycle' does it actually take the time to ask the poor themselves how they perceive their needs [...] the poor are entirely left out of the decision-making progress—almost as if they don't exist."

World Bank and IMF policy is forged in meetings in lavish hotels between people who will never have to live a day in poverty in their lives. As Joseph Stiglitz argues in his own criticism of the World Bank and IMF, "modern high-tech warfare is designed to remove physical contact: dropping bombs from 50,000 feet ensures that one does not 'feel' what one does. Modern economic management is similar: from one's luxury hotel, one can callously impose policies about which one would think twice if one knew the people whose lives one was destroying."[139]

Strikingly, World Bank and IMF leaders are sometimes the very same people who drop the bombs. For example, Robert McNamara—probably the most transformative person in World Bank history,[140] famous for massively expanding its lending and sinking poor countries into inescapable debt—

was first the CEO of the Ford corporation, before becoming U.S. defense secretary, where he sent 500,000 American troops to fight in Vietnam. After leaving the World Bank, he went straight to the board of Royal Dutch Shell.[141] A more recent World Bank head was Paul Wolfowitz, one of the key architects of the Iraq War.

The development set makes its decisions far away from the populations who end up feeling the impact, and they hide the details behind mountains of paperwork, reports, and euphemistic jargon. Like the old British Colonial Office, the set conceals itself "like a cuttlefish, in a cloud of ink."

The prolific and exhausting histories written by the set are hagiographies: The human experience is airbrushed out. A good example is a study called, *Balance of Payments Adjustment, 1945 to 1986: The IMF Experience.*[142] This author had the tedious experience of reading the entire tome. Benefits from colonialism are entirely ignored. The personal stories and human experiences of the people who suffered under World Bank and IMF policies are elided. Hardship is buried under countless charts and statistics. These studies, which dominate the discourse, read as if their main priority is to avoid offending World Bank or IMF staff. Sure, the tone implies that perhaps mistakes were made here or there, but the intentions of the World Bank and IMF are good. They are here to help.

In one example from the aforementioned study, structural adjustment in Argentina in 1959 and 1960 is described as such: "*While the measures had initially reduced the standard of living of a vast sector of the Argentine population*, in relatively short time these measures had resulted in a favorable trade balance and balance of payments, an increase in foreign exchange reserves, a sharp reduction in the rate of increases in the cost of living, a stable exchange rate, and increased domestic and foreign investment."

In layman's terms: Sure, there was enormous impoverishment of the entire population, but hey, we got a better balance sheet, more savings for the regime, and more deals with multinational corporations.

The euphemisms keep coming. Poor countries are consistently described as "test cases." The lexicon and jargon and language of development economics is designed to hide what is actually happening, to mask the cruel reality with terms and process and theory, and to avoid stating the underlying mechanism: rich countries siphoning resources from poor countries and enjoying double standards that enrich their populations while impoverishing people elsewhere.

The apotheosis of the World Bank and IMF's relationship with the developing world is their annual meeting in Washington, DC: a grand festival on poverty in the richest country on earth.

"Over mountainous piles of beautifully prepared food," Hancock writes, "huge volumes of business get done; meanwhile staggering displays of dominance and ostentation get smoothly blended with empty and meaningless rhetoric about the predicament of the poor."

"The 10,000 men and women attending," he writes, "look extraordinarily unlikely to achieve [their] noble objectives; when not yawning or asleep at the plenary sessions they are to be found enjoying a series of cocktail parties, lunches, afternoon teas, dinners, and midnight snacks lavish enough to surfeit the greenest gourmand. The total cost of the 700 social events laid on for delegates during a single week [in 1989] was estimated at $10 million—a sum of money that might, perhaps, have better 'served the needs of the poor' had it been spent in some other way."

This was thirty-three years ago: One can only imagine the cost of these parties in today's dollars.

In his book, *The Fiat Standard*, Saifedean Ammous has a different name for the development set: The misery industry. His description is worth quoting at length:

"When World Bank planning inevitably fails and the debts cannot be repaid, the IMF comes in to shake down the deadbeat countries, pillage their resources, and take control of political institutions. It is a symbiotic relationship between the two parasitic organizations that generates a lot of work, income and travel for the misery industry's workers—at the expense of the poor countries that have to pay for it all in loans."

"The more one reads about it," Ammous writes, "the more one realizes how catastrophic it has been to hand this class of powerful yet unaccountable bureaucrats an endless line of fiat credit and unleash them on the world's poor. This arrangement allows unelected foreigners with nothing at stake to control and centrally plan entire nations' economies […] Indigenous populations are removed from their lands, private businesses are closed to protect monopoly rights, taxes are raised, and property is confiscated […] tax-free deals are provided to international corporations under the auspices of the International Financial Institutions, while local producers pay ever-higher taxes and suffer from inflation to accommodate their governments' fiscal incontinence."

"As part of the debt relief deals signed with the misery industry," he continues, "governments were asked to sell off some of their most prized assets. This included government enterprises, but also national resources and entire swaths of land. The IMF would usually auction these to multinational corporations and negotiate with governments for them to be exempt from local taxes and laws. After decades of saturating the world with easy credit, the IFIs spent the 1980s acting as repo men. They went through the wreckage of third-world countries devastated by their policies and sold whatever was valuable to multinational corporations, giving them protection from the law in the scrap heaps in which they operated. This reverse Robin Hood redistribution was the inevitable consequence of the dynamics created when these organizations were endowed with easy money."

"By ensuring the whole world stays on the U.S. dollar standard," Ammous concludes, "the IMF guarantees the US can continue to operate its inflationary monetary policy and export its inflation globally. Only when one understands the grand larceny at the heart of the global monetary system can one understand the plight of developing countries."

X. WHITE ELEPHANTS

"What Africa needs to do is grow, grow out of debt."

—*George Ayittey*

By the mid-1970s, it was clear to Western policymakers, and especially to World Bank president Robert McNamara, that the only way poor countries would be able to pay back their debt was with more debt.[143]

The IMF had always paired its lending with structural adjustment, but for its first few decades, the World Bank would give project-specific or sector-specific loans with no additional conditions attached. This changed during McNamara's tenure, as less specific structural adjustment loans became popular and then even dominant at the World Bank during the 1980s.

The reason was simple enough: World Bank workers had a lot more money to lend out, and it was easier to give away large sums if the money was not tied to specific projects. As Cheryl Payer notes, "twice as many dollars per staff week of work" could be disbursed through structural adjustment loans.

The borrowers, Graham Hancock says, couldn't be happier: "Corrupt ministers of finance and dictatorial presidents from Asia, Africa, and Latin America tripped over their own expensive footwear in their unseemly haste to get adjusted. For such people, money was probably never easier to obtain: With no complicated projects to administer and no messy accounts to keep, the venal, the cruel, and the ugly laughed literally all the way to the bank. For them structural adjustment was like a dream come true. No sacrifices were demanded of them personally. All they had to do—amazing but true—was screw the poor."

Beyond "general use" structural adjustment loans, the other way to spend large amounts of money was to finance massive, individual projects. These would become known as "white elephants," and their carcasses still dot the deserts, mountains, and forests of the developing world. These behemoths were notorious for their human and environmental devastation.

A good example would be the billion-dollar Inga dams, built in Zaire in 1972, whose World Bank–funded architects electrified the exploitation of the mineral-rich Katanga province, without installing any transformers along the way to help the vast numbers of villagers who were still using oil lamps.[144] Or the Chad–Cameroon pipeline in the 1990s: This $3.7 billion, World Bank–funded project was built entirely to siphon resources out of the ground to enrich the Idriss Déby dictatorship and its foreign collaborators, without any benefits for the people.[145] Between 1979 and 1983, World Bank–financed hydroelectric projects "resulted in the involuntary resettlement of at least 400,000 to 450,000 people on four continents."

Hancock details many such white elephants in *Lords of Poverty*. One example is the Singrauli Power and Coal Mining Complex in India's Uttar Pradesh state, which received nearly a billion dollars in World Bank funding.

Source: Ramkesh Patel Rosehubwiki

The Singrauli coal fields.

"Here," Hancock writes, "because of 'development,' 300,000 poor rural people were subjected to frequent forced relocations as new mines and power stations opened [...] the land was totally destroyed and resembled scenes out of the lower circles of Dante's inferno. Enormous amounts of dust and air and water pollution of every conceivable sort created tremendous public health problems. Tuberculosis was rampant, potable water supplies destroyed, and chloroquine-resistant malaria afflicted the area. Once prosperous villages and hamlets were replaced by unspeakable hovels and shacks on the edges of huge infrastructure projects [...] some people were living inside the open pit mines. Over 70,000 previously self-sufficient peasant farmers—deprived of all over possible sources of income—had no choice but to accept the indignity of intermittent employment at Singrauli for salaries of around 70 cents a day: below survival level even in India."

In Guatemala, Hancock describes a giant hydroelectric dam called the Chixoy, built with World Bank support in the Mayan highlands.

"Originally budgeted at $340 million," he writes, "the construction costs had risen to $1 billion by the time the dam was opened in 1985 [...] the money was lent to the Guatemalan government by a consortium [led] by the World Bank [...] General Romero Lucas Arica's military government, in power during the bulk of the construction phase and which signed the contract with the World Bank, was recognized by political analysts as having been the most corrupt administration in the history of a Central American country in a region that has been afflicted by more than its fair share of venal and dishonest regimes [...] members of the junta pocketed about $350 million out of the $1 billion provided for Chixoy."

As one final example in this chapter, in Brazil, Hancock details one of the World Bank's most harmful projects, a "massive colonization and resettlement scheme," known as Polonoroeste. By 1985, the World Bank had committed $434.3 million to the initiative, which ended up transforming "poor people into refugees in their own land."

The scheme "persuaded hundreds of thousands of needy people to migrate from Brazil's central and southern provinces and relocate themselves as farmers in the Amazon basin" to generate cash crops. "The Bank's money," Hancock wrote, "paid for the speedy paving of Highway BR-364 which runs into the heart of the north-western province of Rondonia. All the settlers traveled along this road on their way to farms that they slashed and burned out of the jungle [...] Already 4% deforested in 1982, Rondonia was 11% deforested by 1985. NASA space surveys showed that the area of deforestation was doubled approximately every two years."

As a result of the project, in 1988 "tropical forests covering an area larger than Belgium were burnt by settlers." Hancock also notes that "more than 200,000 settlers were estimated to have contracted a particularly virulent strain of malaria, endemic in the north-west, to which they had no resistance."

Such grotesque projects were the result of the massive growth of lending institutions, a detachment of the creditors from the actual places they were lending to, and management by unaccountable local autocrats who pocketed billions along the way. They were the outcome of policies that tried to lend as much money as possible to Third World countries to keep the debt Ponzi scheme going and to keep the flow of resources from south to north moving. The grimmest example of all might be found in Indonesia.

XI. A REAL-LIFE PANDORA: THE EXPLOITATION OF WEST PAPUA

"You want a fair deal, you're on the wrong planet."

—*Jake Sully*

The island of New Guinea is resource-rich beyond imagination. It contains, just for starters, the third-largest expanse of tropical rainforest in the world, after the Amazon and the Congo;[146] the world's largest gold and copper mine at Grasberg, in the shadow of the 4,800-meter "Seven Summit" peak of Puncak Jaya; and, offshore, the Coral Triangle, a tropical sea known for its "unparalleled" reef diversity.[147]

And yet, the people of the island, especially those living in the California-sized Western half under Indonesian control, are some of the poorest in the world. Resource colonialism has long been a curse for the residents of this territory, known as West Papua. Whether the pillage was committed by the Dutch, or, in more recent decades, the Indonesian government, imperialists have found generous support from the World Bank and the IMF.

This book has already mentioned how one of the World Bank's first loans was to the Dutch, which it used to try and sustain its colonial empire in Indonesia. In 1962, Imperial Holland was finally defeated and gave up control over West Papua to the Sukarno government as Indonesia became independent.[148] However, the Papuans (also known as the Irianese) wanted their own freedom.

In the course of that decade—as the IMF credited the Indonesian government with more than $100 million— Papuans were purged from positions of leadership. In 1969, in an event that would make George Orwell's Oceania blush, Jakarta held the "Act of Free Choice," a poll where 1,025 people were rounded up and forced to vote in front of armed soldiers.[149] The results to join Indonesia were unanimous, and the vote was ratified by the UN General Assembly.[150] After that, locals had no say in what "development" projects would proceed. Oil, copper, and timber were all harvested and removed from the island in the following decades, with no involvement by Papuans, except as forced labor.[151]

The mines, highways, and ports in West Papua were not built with the well-being of the population in mind, but rather were built to loot the island as efficiently as possible. As Cheryl Payer was able to observe even in 1974, the IMF helped transform Indonesia's vast natural resources into "mortgages for an indefinite future to subsidize an oppressive military dictatorship and to pay for imports which supported the lavish lifestyle of the generals in Jakarta."

A 1959 article on the discovery of gold in the area is the beginning of the story that what would later become the Grasberg mine, the world's lowest-cost and largest producer of copper and gold.[152] In 1972, the Phoenix-based Freeport signed a deal with Indonesian dictator Suharto to extract gold and copper from West Papua, without any consent from the indigenous population. Until 2017, Freeport controlled 90% of the project's shares, with 10% in the hands of the Indonesian government, and 0% for the Amungme and Kamoro tribes who actually inhabit the area.

Source: www.sika.com

The Grasberg mine.

By the time Grasberg's treasures are fully depleted by the Freeport corporation, the project will have generated some 6 billion tons of waste: More than twice as much rock as was excavated to dig the Panama Canal.[153]

The ecosystems downstream from the mine have since been devastated and stripped of life as more than a billion tons of waste have been dumped "directly into a jungle river in what had been one of the world's last untouched landscapes." Satellite reports show the devastation wrought by the ongoing dumping of more than 200,000 of toxic tailings per day into an area that contains the Lorentz National Park, a world heritage site.[154] Freeport remains the largest foreign taxpayer in Indonesia and the biggest employer in West Papua: It plans to stay until 2040, when the gold will run out.[155]

As the World Bank writes candidly in its very own report on the region, "international business interests want better infrastructure in order to extract and export the non-renewable mineral and forest assets."[156]

By far the most shocking program that the World Bank financed in West Papua was "transmigration," a euphemism for settler colonialism. For more than a century, the powers in control of Java (home to most of Indonesia's population) dreamed of moving large chunks of Javanese to farther-flung islands in the archipelago. Not just to spread things out, but also to ideologically "unify" the territory. In a 1985 speech, the Minister of Transmigration said that "by way of transmigration, we will try to […] integrate all the ethnic groups into one nation, the Indonesian nation […] The different ethnic groups will in the long run disappear because of integration […] there will be one kind of man."

These efforts to resettle Javanese—known as *Transmigrasi*   began during colonial times, but in the 1970s and 1980s, the World Bank began financing these activities in an aggressive way. The World Bank allocated hundreds of millions of dollars to the Suharto dictatorship to allow it to "transmigrate" what were hoped to be millions of people to places like East Timor and West Papua in what was "the world's largest-ever exercise in human resettlement." By 1986, the World Bank had committed no less than $600 million directly to support transmigration, which entailed "a breathtaking combination of human rights abuses and environmental destruction."

Consider the story of the Sago palm, one of the main traditional food stuffs of Papuans.[157] One tree alone was able to supply food for a family for six to twelve months. But the Indonesian government, at the encouragement of the World Bank, came and said no, this is not working: You need to eat rice. So, the Sago gardens were cut down to grow rice for export; and the locals were forced to buy rice in the market, which simply made them more dependent on Jakarta.

Any resistance was met with brutality. Especially under Suharto—who held as many as 100,000 political prisoners—but even today, in 2022, West Papua is a police state almost without rival.[158] Foreign journalists are virtually banned; free speech does not exist; the military operates without any accountability. Non-governmental organizations, like Tapol,[159] document a legion of human rights violations, ranging from mass surveillance of personal devices, restrictions on when and for what reason people can leave their homes, and even rules on how Papuans can wear their hair.[160]

Between 1979 and 1984, some 59,700 transmigrants
were taken to West Papua, with "large scale" support from the
World Bank. More than 20,000 Papuans fled the violence into
neighboring Papua New Guinea. Refugees reported to
international media that "their villages were bombed, their
settlements burned, women raped, livestock killed, and
numbers of people indiscriminately shot while others were
imprisoned and tortured."

A subsequent project backed by a $160 million World
Bank loan in 1985 was called "Transmigration V": The
seventh World Bank–funded project in support of settler
colonialism, it aimed to finance the relocation of 300,000
families between 1986 and 1992.[161] The regime's governor of
West Papua at the time described the indigenous people as
"living in a stone-age era" and called for a further 2 million
Javanese migrants to be sent to the islands so that "backwards
local people could intermarry with the newcomers thus giving
birth to a new generation of people without curly hair."

The original and final versions of the Transmigration V
loan agreement were leaked to Survival International: The
original version made "extensive reference to the bank's
policies on tribal peoples and provides a list of measures that
would be required to comply with these," but the final version
made "no reference to the bank's policies."[162]

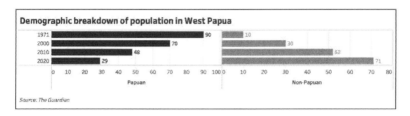

Cultural genocide in West Papua.

Transmigration V ran into budget issues and was cut short, but ultimately, 161,600 families were moved, at a cost of 14,146 World Bank staff months. The World Bank was clearly financing cultural genocide: Today, Ethnic Papuans make up no more than 30% of the territory's population.[163] But social engineering wasn't the only goal of taking money from the World Bank; 17% of funds for transmigration projects were estimated to have been stolen by government officials.[164]

Fifteen years later, on December 11, 2001, the World Bank approved a $200 million loan to "improve road conditions" in West Papua and other parts of Eastern Indonesia. [165] The project, known as EIRTP, aimed to "improve the condition of national and other strategic arterial roads in order to reduce transport costs and provide more reliable access among provincial centers, regional development and production areas, and other key transport facilities. Reducing road transport costs," the World Bank said, "will help to lower input prices, raise output prices and increase the competitiveness of local products from the affected areas." In other words: The World Bank was helping to extract resources as efficiently as possible.

The World Bank and IMF's history in Indonesia is so outrageous that it seems like it must be from another time, ages ago. But that's simply not true. Between 2003 and 2008, the World Bank funded palm oil development in Indonesia to the tune of nearly $200 million and hired private companies who were alleged to have "used fire to clear primary forests and seize lands belonging to indigenous people without due process."[166]

In 2023, the Indonesian government remains on the hook for the EIRTP loan. In the past five years, the World Bank has collected $70 million in interest payments from the Indonesian government and taxpayer, all for its efforts to accelerate the extraction of resources from islands like West Papua.[167]

XII. THE WORLD'S BIGGEST PONZI

"Countries don't go bankrupt."

—*Walter Wriston,*

Former Chairman of Citibank

One might consider bankruptcy an important and even essential part of capitalism. But the IMF basically exists to prevent the free market from working as it normally would: It bails out countries that normally would go bankrupt, forcing them instead deeper into debt.

The IMF makes the impossible possible: Small, poor countries hold so much debt that they could never pay it all off. These bailouts corrupt the incentives of the global financial system. In a true free market, there would be serious consequences for risky lending: The creditor bank could lose its money.

When the United States, Europe, or Japan made their deposits at the World Bank and IMF, it was similar to purchasing insurance on their ability to extract wealth from developing nations. Their private banks and multinational corporations are protected by the bailout scheme, and on top of it, they earn handsome, steady interest (paid for by poor countries) on what is widely perceived to be humanitarian assistance.

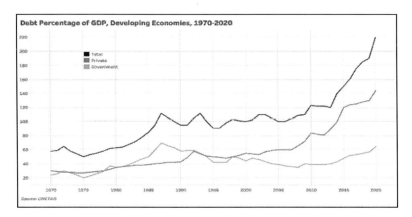

The exponential rise of Third World debt.

As David Graeber writes in *Debt*, when banks "lent money to dictators in Bolivia and Gabon in the late '70s: [they made] utterly irresponsible loans with the full knowledge that, once it became known they had done so, politicians and bureaucrats would scramble to ensure that they'd still be reimbursed anyway, no matter how many lives had to be devastated and destroyed in order to do it."

Kevin Danaher describes the tension that began to emerge in the 1960s: "Borrowers began to pay back more annually to the Bank than it disbursed in new loans. In 1963, 1964, and 1969 India transferred more money to the World Bank than the Bank disbursed to it." Technically, India was paying off its debts plus interest, but the World Bank's leadership saw a crisis.

"To solve the problem," Danaher continues, World Bank President Robert McNamara increased lending "at a phenomenal rate, from $953 million in 1968 to $12.4 billion in 1981." The number of IMF lending programs also "more than doubled" from 1976 to 1983, mostly to poor countries.[168] The World Bank and the IMF's assurances led the world's titanic money center banks, as well as hundreds of regional and local banks in the United States and Europe—"most of them with little or no previous history of foreign lending"—to go on an unprecedented lending spree.

The Third World debt bubble finally burst in 1982, when Mexico announced a default. According to official IMF history, "private bankers envisaged the dreaded possibility of a widespread repudiation of debts, such as had occurred in the 1930s: at that time the debt owed by debtor countries to industrial counties was mostly in the form of securities issued by debtor countries in the US and in the form of bonds sold abroad; in the 1980s the debt was almost entirely in the form of short- and medium- term loans from commercial banks in the industrial members. Monetary authorities of industrial members instantly realized the urgency of the problem posed for the world's banking system."[169]

In other words, the threat that the banks of the West might have holes on their balance sheet was the danger: *Not* that millions would die of austerity programs in poor countries. In her book, *A Fate Worse Than Debt*, the development critic Susan George charts how the top-nine, largest, U.S. banks all had placed more than 100% of their shareholders' equity in "loans to Mexico, Brazil, Argentina, and Venezuela alone." The crisis was averted, however, as the IMF helped credit flow to Third World countries, even though they should have gone bankrupt.

"Simply put," according to a technical analysis of the IMF, its programs "provide bailouts for private lenders to emerging markets, thereby allowing international creditors to benefit from foreign lending without bearing the full risks involved: the banks reap significant profits if borrowers repay their debts and avoid losses if financial crisis occur."[170]

Latin American citizens suffered under structural adjustment, but between 1982 and 1985. Susan George reported that "in spite of over-exposure to Latin America, dividends declared by the big nine banks increased by more than a third during the same period."[171] Profits in that time rose by 84% at Chase Manhattan and 66% at World Banker's Trust, and stock value rose by 86% at Chase and 83% at Citicorp.

"Clearly," she wrote, "austerity is not the term to describe the experiences since 1982 of either the Third World elite or the international banks: the parties that contracted the loans in the first place."

The "generosity" of the West enabled unaccountable leaders to plunge their nations into debt deeper than ever before. The system was, as Cheryl Payer writes in *Lent and Lost*, a straightforward Ponzi scheme: The new loans went straight to paying for the old loans. The system needed to grow to avoid collapse.

"By keeping financing going," an IMF managing director said, according to Payer, structural adjustment loans "permitted trade that might otherwise not have been possible."

Given that the World Bank and IMF will prevent even the most comically corrupt and wasteful governments from going bankrupt, private banks adapted their behavior accordingly. A good example would be Argentina, which has received twenty-two IMF loans since 1959, even trying to default in 2001.[172] One would think that creditors would stop lending to such a profligate borrower. But in fact, just four years ago, Argentina received the largest IMF loan of all time, a staggering $57.1 billion.[173]

Payer summed up *The Debt Trap* by stating that the moral of her work was "both simple and old-fashioned: That nations, like individuals, cannot spend more than they earn without falling into debt, and a heavy debt burden bars the way to autonomous action."

But the system makes the deal too sweet for the creditors: Profits are monopolized while losses are socialized.

Payer realized this even fifty years ago in 1974, and hence concluded that "in the long run it is more realistic to withdraw from an exploitative system and suffer the dislocation of readjustment than it is to petition the exploiters for a degree of relief."

XIII. DO AS I SAY, NOT AS I DO

"Our lifestyle is not up for negotiation."

—*George H.W. Bush*

In a true global free market, the neoliberal policies that the World Bank and IMF impose on poor countries might make sense. After all, the record of socialism and large-scale nationalization of industry is disastrous. The problem is, the world is not a free market, and double standards are everywhere.

Subsidies—for example, free rice in Sri Lanka or discounted fuel in Nigeria—are ended by the IMF, yet creditor nations like the United Kingdom and United States extend state-funded healthcare[174] and crop subsidies to their own populations.[175]

One can take a Libertarian or Marxist view and arrive at the same conclusion: This is a double standard which enriches some countries at the expense of others, with most citizens of rich countries blissfully unaware.

To help build out from the rubble of World War II, IMF creditors relied heavily on central planning and anti-free market policy for the first few decades after Bretton

Woods:[176] For example, import restrictions, capital outflow limits, foreign exchange caps, and crop subsidies. These measures protected industrial economies when they were most vulnerable.[177]

In the United States, for example, the Interest Equalization Act was passed by John F. Kennedy to stop Americans from buying foreign securities and instead focus them on domestic investing.[178] This was one of many measures to tighten capital controls. But the World Bank and IMF have historically prevented poor countries from using the same tactics to defend themselves.

As Cheryl Payer observes, "The IMF has never played a deciding role in the adjustment of exchange rates and trade practices among the wealthy developed nations […] It is the weaker nations which are subjected to the full force of the IMF principles […] the inequality of power relationships meant that the IMF could do nothing about market 'distortions' (such as trade protection) which were practiced by the rich countries."

Cato's Vásquez and Bandow came to a similar conclusion, noting that "most industrialized nations have maintained a patronizing attitude towards underdeveloped nations, hypocritically shutting out their exports."

In the early 1990s, while the United States stressed the importance of free trade, it "erected a virtual iron curtain against [Eastern Europe's] exports, including textiles, steel, and agricultural products." Poland, Czechoslovakia, Hungary, Romania, Bosnia, Croatia, Slovenia, Azerbaijan, Belarus,

Georgia, Kazakhstan, Kyrgyzstan, Moldova, Russia, Tajikistan, Turkmenistan, Ukraine, and Uzbekistan were all targeted. The United States prevented Eastern European nations from selling "a single pound of butter, dry milk, or ice cream in America" and both the Bush and Clinton administrations imposed stiff chemical and pharmaceutical import restrictions on the region.

It is estimated that protectionism by industrial countries "reduces developing countries' national income by roughly twice as much as provided by development assistance." In other words, if Western nations simply opened their economies, they wouldn't have to provide any development assistance at all.

There is a sinister twist to the arrangement: When a Western country (i.e., the United States) runs into an inflationary crisis—like today's—and is forced to tighten its monetary policy, it actually *gains more control* over developing countries and their resources, whose dollar debt becomes much more difficult to pay back, and who fall deeper into the debt trap, and deeper into World Bank and IMF conditionality.

In 2008, during the Great Financial Crisis, American and European authorities lowered interest rates and juiced up banks with extra cash.[179] During the Third World Debt Crisis and the Asian Financial Crisis, the World Bank and IMF refused to permit this kind of behavior. Instead, the recommendation to afflicted economies was to tighten at home and borrow more from abroad.[180]

In September 2022, newspaper headlines stated that the IMF was "worried" about inflation in the United Kingdom, as its bond market teetered on the brink of collapse.[181] This is, of course, another hypocrisy, given that the IMF did not seem worried about inflation when it imposed currency devaluation on billions of people for decades. Creditor nations play by different rules.

In a final case of "do as I say, not as I do," the IMF still holds a whopping 90.5 million ounces—or 2,814 metric tons—of gold. Most of this was accumulated in the 1940s, when members were forced to pay 25% of their original quotas in gold. In fact, until the 1970s, members "normally paid all interest owed on IMF credit in gold."[182]

When Richard Nixon formally ended the gold standard in 1971, the IMF did not sell its gold reserves. And yet, attempts by any member countries to fix their currency to gold are forbidden.[183]

XIV. GREEN COLONIALISM

"If you turned the electricity off for a few months in any developed Western society, 500 years of supposed philosophical progress about human rights and individualism would quickly evaporate like they never happened."

—*Murtaza Hussain*

In the past few decades, a new double standard has emerged: green colonialism. This, at least, is what the Senegalese entrepreneur Magatte Wade calls the West's hypocrisy over energy use.

In an interview for this book, Wade explained that industrial countries developed their civilizations by utilizing hydrocarbons (in large part stolen or bought on the cheap from poor countries or colonies), but today, the World Bank and IMF try to push policies which prohibit the developing world from doing the same.

Where the United States and United Kingdom were able to use coal and the Third World's oil, the World Bank and IMF want African countries to use solar and wind manufactured and financed by the West.

This hypocrisy was on display in late 2022 in Egypt, where world leaders gathered at COP 27 (the Sharm el-Sheikh Climate Change Conference) to discuss how to reduce energy use. The location on the African continent was intentional.[184] Western leaders—currently scrambling to import more fossil fuels after their access to Russian hydrocarbons was curtailed—flew in on gas-guzzling private jets to plead with poor countries to reduce their carbon footprint. In typical World Bank and IMF tradition, the ceremonies were hosted by the resident military dictator. During the festivities, Alaa Abd Al Fattah, a prominent Egyptian human rights activist, languished nearby on hunger strike in prison.

Source: REUTERS / Alamy Stock Photo/POOL

British Prime Minister Rishi Sunak arrives at COP 27 on a private jet.

"Just like back in the day when we were colonized and the colonizers set the rules to how our societies would work," Wade said, "this green agenda is a new form of governing us. This is master now dictating to us what our relationship with energy should be, telling us what kind of energy we should use, and when we can use it. The oil is in our soil, it is part of our sovereignty: but now they are saying we cannot use it? Even after they looted incalculable amounts for themselves?"

Wade points out that as soon as the core countries have an economic crisis (as they faced in 2022), they go right back to using fossil fuels. She observes that poor countries aren't allowed to develop nuclear energy, and notes that when Third World leaders tried to push in this direction in the past, some of them—notably in Pakistan[185] and Brazil[186]—were assassinated.

Wade says her life's work is prosperity building in Africa. She was born in Senegal and moved to Germany at age seven. She still remembers her first day in Europe. She was used to a shower being a thirty-minute affair: get the coal stove going, boil the water, put some cold water in it to cool it down, and drag the water to the shower area. But in Germany, all she had to do was turn a handle.

"I was shocked," she says. "This question defined the rest of my life: How come they have this here but we don't over there?"

Wade learned over time that reasons for Western success included the rule of law, clear and transferable property rights, and stable currencies. But, also, critically, reliable energy access.

"We can't have limitations on our energy use imposed on us by others," Wade said. And yet, the World Bank and IMF continue to put pressure on energy policy in poor countries. In October 2022, Haiti followed pressure from the World Bank and IMF to end its fuel subsidies. "The result," wrote energy reporter Michael Schellenberger, "has been riots, looting, and chaos."[187]

"In 2018," Schellenberger says, "the Haitian government agreed to IMF demands that it cut fuel subsidies as a prerequisite for receiving $96 million from the World Bank, European Union, and Inter-American Development bank, triggering protests that resulted in the resignation of the prime minister."

"In over 40 nations since 2005," he says, "riots have been triggered after cutting fuel subsidies or otherwise raising energy prices."

It is the height of hypocrisy for the West to achieve success based on robust energy consumption and on energy subsidies, and then try to limit the type and amount of energy used by poor countries, and then raise the price that their citizens pay. This amounts to a Malthusian scheme in line with former World Bank chief Robert McNamara's well-documented belief that population growth was a threat to humanity. The solution, of course, was always to try and reduce the population of poor countries, not rich ones.[188]

"They treat us like little experiments," Wade says, "where the West says: We might lose some people along the way, but let's see if poor countries can develop without the energy types we used."

"Well," she says, "we are not an experiment."

XV. THE HUMAN TOLL OF STRUCTURAL ADJUSTMENT

*"To the World Bank, development means growth [...] But [...]
unrestrained growth is the ideology of the cancer cell."*

—*Mohammed Yunus*

The social impact of structural adjustment is immense, and barely ever gets mentioned in traditional analysis of the World Bank and IMF's policy. There have been plenty of exhaustive studies done on their economic impact, but very little comparatively on their global health impact.

Researchers like George Ayittey, Graham Hancock, and Cheryl Payer give a few jarring examples from the 1970s and 1980s:

• Between 1977 and 1985, Peru undertook IMF structural adjustment: The average-per-capita income of Peruvians fell 20%, and inflation soared from 30% to 160%. By 1985, a worker's pay was only worth 64% of what it had been worth in 1979 and 44% of what it had been in 1973. Child malnutrition rose from 42% to 68% of the population.

• In 1984 and 1985, the Philippines under Marcos implemented yet another round of IMF structural reform: After a year, gross domestic product per capita regressed to

1975 levels. Real earnings fell by 46% among urban wage earners.

• In Sri Lanka, the poorest 30% suffered an uninterrupted decline in calorie consumption after more than a decade of structural adjustment.

• In Brazil, the number of citizens suffering from malnutrition jumped from 27 million (one third of the population) in 1961 to 86 million (two thirds of the population) in 1985 after ten doses of structural adjustment.

• Between 1975 and 1984, in IMF-guided Bolivia, the number of hours the average citizen had to work to purchase 1,000 calories of bread, beans, corn, wheat, sugar, potatoes, milk, or quinoa increased on average by five times.

• After structural adjustment in Jamaica in 1984, the nutritional purchasing power of one Jamaican dollar plummeted in fourteen months from being able to buy 2,232 calories of flour to just 1,443; from 1,649 calories of rice to 905; from 1,037 calories of condensed milk to 508; and from 220 calories of chicken to 174.

• As a result of structural adjustment, Mexican real wages declined in the 1980s by more than 75%. In 1986, about 70% of lower-income Mexicans had "virtually stopped eating rice, eggs, fruit, vegetables, and milk (never mind meat or fish)" at a time when their government was paying $27 million per day—$18,750 per minute—in interest to its creditors. By the 1990s, "a family of four on the minimum wage (which made up 60% of the employed labor force) could only buy 25% of its basic needs.

• In the twenty years following India's 1992 structural adjustment, the percent of the rural population that lived without the bare minimum of calories increased from 75% to 91%.[189]

• In sub-Saharan Africa, GNP per capita "dropped steadily from $624 in 1980 to $513 in 1998 [...] food production per capita in Africa was 105 in 1980 but 92 for 1997 [...] and food imports rose an astonishing 65% between 1988 and 1997."

These examples, though tragic, only give a small and patchwork picture of the deleterious impact that World Bank and IMF policies have had on the health of the world's poor.

On average, every year from 1980 to 1985, there were forty-seven countries in the Third World pursuing IMF-sponsored structural adjustment programs, and twenty-one developing countries pursuing structural or sector adjustment loans from the World Bank. During this same period, 75% of all countries in Latin America and Africa experienced declines in per capita income and child welfare. The amount of food that an unskilled worker's daily wage could purchase fell back to levels not seen since the seventeenth and eighteenth centuries.[190]

The decline in living standards makes sense when one considers that World Bank and IMF policies sculpted societies to focus on exports at the expense of consumption while gutting food security and healthcare services.

During IMF structural adjustment, real wages in countries like Kenya declined by more than 40%. After billions in World Bank and IMF credit, per capita food production in Africa fell by nearly 20% between 1960 and 1994. Meanwhile, health expenditures in "IMF-World World Bank programmed countries" declined by 50% during the 1980s.

When food security and healthcare collapse, people die.

Papers from 2011 and 2013 showed that countries that took a structural adjustment loan had higher levels of child mortality than those that did not.[191] A 2017 analysis was "virtually unanimous in finding a detrimental association between structural adjustment and child and maternal health outcomes."[192] A 2020 study reviewed data from 137 developing countries between 1980 and 2014 and found that "structural adjustment reforms lower health system access and increase neonatal mortality."[193] A paper from 2021 concluded that structural adjustment plays "a significant role in perpetuating preventable disability and death."[194]

It is impossible to do a full accounting of just how many women, men, and children were killed as a result of World Bank and IMF austerity policies.

Food security advocate Davidson Budhoo claimed that 6 million children died each year in Africa, Asia, and Latin America between 1982 and 1994, as a result of structural adjustment. This would put the World Bank and IMF's death toll in the same ballpark as the deaths caused by Stalin and Mao.

Is this remotely possible? No one will ever know. But by looking at the data, we can begin to get a sense.

Research from Mexico—a typical country in terms of consistent involvement historically from the World Bank and IMF—shows that for every 2% decrease in GDP, the mortality rate increased by 1%.[195]

Now, consider that as a result of structural adjustment, the GDP of dozens of countries in the Third World between the 1960s and 1990s suffered double-digit contractions. Despite massive population growth, many of these economies stagnated or shrank over fifteen-to-twenty-five-year periods. Meaning, the World Bank and the IMF's policies likely killed tens of millions of people.

Whatever the final death toll, there are two certainties: One, these are crimes against humanity, and two, no World Bank or IMF officials will ever go to prison. There will never be any accountability or justice.

The inescapable reality is that millions died too young in order to extend and improve the lives of millions elsewhere. It is, of course, true that much of the success of the West is because of enlightenment values like rule of law, free speech, liberal democracy, and domestic respect for human rights. But the unspoken truth is that much of the West's success is also the result of resource and time theft from poor countries.

The cycle continues today. According to a 2023 study in BMJ's global health journal, austerity is "on the agenda for 59 out of 125 low-income and middle-income countries by 2024," exposing 2 billion people to health risks.[196] The data shows that low- and middle-income countries spent more in 2022 on external debt repayments than on health programs. Of that external debt, 61% is held by low- and middle-income countries and is owed to Western private sector creditors, who, of course, oppose "any modicum of debt restructuring that would affect the return on their investments."

The stolen wealth and labor of the Third World will go unpunished but remains visible today, forever encrusted in the developed world's architecture, culture, science, technology, and quality of life. The next time one visits London, New York, Tokyo, Paris, Amsterdam, or Berlin, this author suggests going for a walk and pausing at a particularly impressive or scenic view of the city to reflect on this. As the old saying goes, "We must pass through the darkness to reach the light."

XVI. A TRILLION DOLLARS: THE BANK AND FUND IN THE POST-COVID WORLD

"We are all in this together."

—*Christine Lagarde,*
Former IMF Managing Director

World Bank and IMF policy towards developing countries has not changed much over the past few decades. There have been a few superficial tweaks, like the "Heavily Indebted Poor Countries" (HIPC) initiative, where some governments can receive debt relief. But to qualify, these poorest of the poor countries still need to do structural adjustment, now rebranded to "Poverty Reduction Strategy."[197]

The same old rules still apply: In Guyana, for example, "the government decided in early 2000 to increase the salaries of civil servants by 3.5%, after a fall in purchasing power of 30% over the previous five years." The IMF immediately threatened to remove Guyana from the new list of HIPCs. "After a few months, the government had to backpedal."

The same large-scale devastation still occurs. In a 2015 ICIJ report, for instance, it was estimated that 3.4 million people were displaced in the previous decade by World Bank–funded projects.[198]

The old accounting games, meant to exaggerate the good done by assistance, are joined by new ones. The U.S. government applies a 92% discount to the debt of HIPCs, and yet U.S. authorities include the *nominal* value of the debt relief in their "ODA" (official development assistance) numbers. Meaning, America significantly exaggerates the volume of what is seen as charity. The *Financial Times* has argued that ODA is "the aid that isn't" and says that "writing off official commercial debt should not count as aid."

While it's true that there have actually been large transformations at the World Bank and IMF in recent years, those changes have not been in the way that these institutions try to shape the economies of borrowing countries, but rather in that they have focused their efforts on nations closer to the world's economic core.

"By practically any metric," a NBER study observes, "the post-2008 IMF programs to several European economies are the largest in the IMF's 70-year history."[199]

"IMF commitments as a share of world GDP," the study explains, "hit an all-time high as the European Debt Crisis began to unravel." Iceland began an IMF program in 2008, followed by Greece, Ireland, and Portugal.

The IMF-led bailout of Greece was a staggering $375 billion.[200] In July 2015, "popular discontent led to a 'no' vote in a referendum on whether to accept the IMF's loan conditions, which included raising taxes, lowering pensions and other spending, and privatizing industries."[201]

Largest IMF Programs

Country, program year	In million 2009 US$	Percent of GDP	Percent of Quota
Argentina 2018	48,700	11	1,839
Brazil 2002	41,677	7	902
Greece 2010	39,851	14	3,212
Portugal 2011	36,326	16	2,306
Greece 2012	34,700	15	2,159
Ireland 2010	29,347	14	2,322
Korea 1997	27,309	4	1,938
Argentina 2000	27,280	6	800
Turkey 1999	25,674	8	1,560
Russian Fed. 1996	24,976	5	306
Mexico 1995	24,284	5	688
Turkey 2002	19,519	7	1,330
Brazil 2001	18,454	3	400
Brazil 1998	17,912	2	480
Romania 2009	17,645	11	1,111
Ukraine 2008	17,518	10	802
Hungary 2008	16,783	11	1,015
Ukraine 2010	15,076	11	729
Indonesia 1997	14,690	5	557
Argentina 2003	14,504	8	424
India 1981	12,115	3	291
Pakistan 2008	11,524	7	700
United Kingdom 1977	11,146	2	120
Turkey 2005	10,697	2	691

Source: The IMF: 70 Years of Reinvention

The largest IMF bailouts in history.

In the end, however, the Greek people's voice wasn't heard since "the government subsequently ignored the results and accepted the loans."

The IMF used the same playbook in Greece and other lower-income European countries as it has used all over the developing world for decades: It breaks democratic norms to provide billions to the elites, with austerity for the masses.

In the past two years, the World Bank and IMF have pumped hundreds of billions of dollars into countries following government lockdowns and COVID-19 pandemic restrictions. More loans were given out in a shorter time than ever before.[202]

Even in late 2022, as interest rates continue to rise, the debt of poor countries keeps rising, and the amount they owe to rich countries keeps growing. According to the *Financial Times*, "69 low and middle-income countries will make payments of $62 billion" in 2022, a 35% increase from the previous year. History rhymes, and IMF visits to dozens of countries remind us of the early 1980s, when a massive debt bubble was popped by Federal Reserve policies. What followed was the worst depression in the Third World since the 1930s.[203]

We can hope that this does not happen again, but given the World Bank and the IMF's efforts to load up poor countries with more debt than ever before, and given that the cost of borrowing is going up in a historic way, we can predict that it will happen again.

Even where the World Bank and IMF's influence shrinks, the Chinese Communist Party (CCP) is beginning to step in. In the past decade, China has tried to emulate the dynamics of the IMF and World Bank through its own development institutions and through its "Belt and Road" initiative.[204]

As the Indian geostrategist Brahma Chellaney writes, "Through its $1 trillion 'one belt, one road' initiative, China is supporting infrastructure projects in strategically located developing countries, often by extending huge loans to their governments. As a result, countries are becoming ensnared in a debt trap that leaves them vulnerable to China's influence [...] the projects that China is supporting are often intended not to support the local economy, but to facilitate Chinese access to natural resources, or to open the market for its low-cost and shoddy export goods. In many cases, China even sends its own construction workers, minimizing the number of local jobs that are created."[205]

According to the World Bank, the seventy-four poorest countries will owe $35 billion in debt service in 2022.[206] Of that, 37%—around $13.1 billion—will be owed to institutions controlled by the CCP. According to *Banking on Beijing* author Brad Parks, the CCP is now the single-largest lender to the developing world, spanning $843 billion across more than 165 countries and 13,400 projects.[207] Beijing is deploying roughly $85 billion per year to the Global South, and 90% is credit.

The last thing the world needs is another World Bank and IMF drain dynamic, only pulling resources from poor countries to go to the genocidal dictatorship in Beijing. What's worse, many Chinese loan amounts boomerang right back to Beijing as they are immediately used to hire Chinese companies to build infrastructure.[208] It's the same dreaded "double loan" tactic historically used by Western imperial powers. The CCP's goal, over time, is to get developing countries to export to China and accept yuan in return, which they would increasingly use to pay back RMB-denominated loans. It's a new "debt trap," just with a different name.

So, it is good to see the CCP encountering trouble in this area. It is trying to grow its Asian Infrastructure Investment Bank by more than $10 billion per year, but it is encountering a variety of issues with projects that it financed across the developing world. Some governments, like in Sri Lanka, simply cannot pay back.[209] Since the CCP cannot mint the world reserve currency, it actually has to eat the loss. Because of this, it won't likely be able to sustain for decades the lending volume of the United States-Europe-Japan–led system.

Which is certainly a good thing: CCP loans may not come with onerous structural adjustment conditions, but they certainly don't have any considerations for human rights. In fact, the CCP helped shield one belt and road client—Sri Lankan President Mahinda Rajapaksa—from war crimes allegations at the United Nations. If a country diplomatically recognizes Taiwan, it becomes automatically ineligible for Chinese credit.[210] Looking at its projects in Southeast Asia (where it is depleting Burmese minerals and timber and eroding Pakistani sovereignty)[211] and sub-Saharan Africa (where it is extracting an enormous number of rare earths),[212] it largely amounts to the same kind of resource theft and geopolitical control tactics practiced by colonial powers for centuries, just dressed up in a new kind of clothing.

It's not clear that the World Bank and IMF even view the CCP as a bad actor. After all, Wall Street and Silicon Valley tend to be quite friendly with the world's worst dictators. China remains a creditor at the World Bank and IMF: Its membership has never been in question, despite the genocide of the Uyghur people. As long as the CCP does not get in the way of the big picture goals, the World Bank and IMF probably don't mind. There's enough loot to go around.

XVII. FROM ARUSHA TO ACCRA

"Those who wield power control money."

—*Arusha Delegates, 1979*

In 1979, developing nations gathered in the Tanzanian city of Arusha to devise an alternative plan to the IMF- and World Bank–led structural adjustment that had left them with mountains of debt and very little say as to the future of the world economy.[213]

"Those who wield power control money," the delegates wrote. "Those who manage and control money wield power. An international monetary system is both a function and an instrument of prevailing power structures."[214]

As Stefan Eich writes in *The Currency of Politics*, "the Arusha Initiative's emphasis on the international monetary system's burden of hierarchical imbalances was a powerful attempt to insist on money's political nature by countering claims to neutral technical expertise asserted by the IMF's money doctors."

"The IMF may have claimed a neutral, objective, scientific stance," Eich writes, "but all scholarly evidence, including the IMF's internal documentation, pointed the other way. The IMF was, in fact, deeply ideological in the way it framed underdevelopment as a lack of private markets but systematically applied double standards in ignoring similar market controls in 'developed' countries."

This resonates with what Cheryl Payer observed, that World Bank and IMF economists "erected a mystique around their subject which intimidated even other economists."

"They represent themselves," she said, "as highly trained technicians who determine the 'correct' exchange rate and 'proper' amount of money creation on the basis of complex formulas. They deny the political significance of their work."

Like most of the leftist discourse on the World Bank and IMF, the criticisms made at Arusha were mostly on target: The institutions were exploitative, and enriched their creditors at the expense of poor countries. But Arusha's solutions missed the mark: central planning, social engineering, and nationalization.

The Arusha delegates advocated for the World Bank and IMF to be abolished, and for odious debts to be canceled, perhaps noble but entirely unrealistic goals. Beyond that, their best plan of action was "shift power into the hands of local governments"; a poor solution given that the vast majority of Third World countries were dictatorships.

For decades, the public in developing countries suffered as their leaders wavered between selling out their country to multinational corporations and socialist authoritarianism. Both options were destructive.

This is the trap that Ghana has found itself in since independence from the British Empire. More often than not, the Ghanaian authorities, regardless of ideology, chose the option of borrowing from abroad.

Ghana has a stereotypical history with the World Bank and IMF:[215]

• military leaders seizing power by coup only to impose IMF structural adjustment;

• real wages dropping between 1971 and 1982 by 82%, with public health spending shrinking 90% and meat prices up 400% during the same time;

• borrowing from the World Bank to build enormous white elephant projects like the Akosombo Dam, which powered a U.S.-owned aluminum plant at the expense of more than 150,000 people who contracted river blindness and paralysis from the creation of the world's largest manmade lake;

• and a depletion of 75% of the country's rainforests as timber, cocoa and minerals industries boomed while domestic food production cratered.

In 2022, $2.2 billion of assistance flowed into Ghana, but the debt stands at an all-time high of $31 billion, up from $750 million fifty years ago.[216]

Since 1982, under IMF "guidance," the Ghanaian cedi was devalued by 38,000%. One of the biggest outcomes of structural adjustment has been, like elsewhere around the world, expedition of the extraction of Ghana's natural resources. Between 1990 and 2002, for example, the government only received $87.3 million from the $5.2 billion worth of gold mined out of Ghanaian soil: In other words, 98.4% of the profits from gold mining in Ghana went to foreigners.[217]

As Ghanaian protestor Lyle Pratt says, "The IMF is not here to bring down prices, they are not here to ensure that we construct roads—it is not their business and they simply don't care […] The IMF's primary concern is to make sure that we build the capacity to pay our loans, not to develop."

Today feels like a rerun. The Ghanaian cedi was one of the world's worst-performing currencies, losing more than half of its value in 2022. The country is facing a debt crisis, and, like in decades past, is forced to prioritize paying back its creditors over investing in its own people.[218]

In October 2022, the country received its latest IMF visit. If a loan is finalized, it would be the seventeenth IMF loan for Ghana since the CIA-backed military coup of 1966. That is *seventeen layers* of structural adjustment.[219] Two months later, the Ghanaian government actually halted payments on some of its external debt, but the $3.4 billion owed to the IMF and the $4.7 billion owed to the World Bank remain on schedule to be paid out.[220]

A visit from the IMF is a bit like a visit from the Grim Reaper—it can only mean one thing: more austerity, pain, and—without exaggeration—death. Perhaps the wealthy and well-connected can escape unscathed or even enriched, but for the poor and working classes, the currency devaluation, rising interest rates, and disappearance of bank credit is devastating. This is not the Ghana of 1973 that Payer first wrote about in *The Debt Trap*: It is fifty years later, and the trap is forty times deeper.[221]

But perhaps there is a glimmer of hope.

On December 5 to 7, 2022, in the Ghanaian capital of Accra, there was a different kind of visit. Instead of creditors looking to charge interest on the people of Ghana and dictate their industries, the speakers and organizers of the Africa Bitcoin Conference gathered to share information, open-source tools, and decentralizing tactics on how to build economic activity beyond the control of corrupt governments and foreign multinational corporations.[222]

Farida Nabourema was the lead organizer. She is pro-democracy, pro-poor, anti-World Bank and IMF, anti-authoritarian, and pro-Bitcoin. In her keynote speech, she decried the colonial financial framework that still exists in Africa, where the vast majority are excluded or left out.[223] Other speakers mentioned that 80% of inter-African flows pass through an American or European intermediary, causing the loss of billions of dollars of local capital to foreign powers.[224]

"The real issue," Payer once wrote, "is *who controls* the capital and technology that is exported to the poorer countries."

One can argue that Bitcoin as capital and as technology is being exported to Ghana and Togo: It certainly didn't arise there. But it's not clear where it arose. No one knows who created it. And no government or corporation can control it.

During the gold standard, the violence of colonialism corrupted a neutral monetary standard. In the post-colonial world, a fiat monetary standard—upheld by the World Bank and IMF—corrupted a post-colonial power structure. For the Third World, perhaps a post-colonial, post-fiat world will be the right mix.

Proponents of dependency theory like Samir Amin gathered at conferences like Arusha and called for a "delinking" of poor countries from rich ones.[225] The idea was that the wealth of rich countries was not just attributable to their liberal democracies, property rights, and entrepreneurial environments, but also to their resource and labor theft from poor countries. Sever that drain, and poor countries could get a leg up. Amin predicted that "the construction of a system beyond capitalism will have to begin in the peripheral areas."[226] If we agree with Allen Farrington that today's fiat system is not capitalism, and that the current dollar system is deeply flawed, then perhaps Amin was right. A new system is more likely to emerge in Accra, not Washington or London.[227]

As Saifedean Ammous writes, "The developing world consists of countries that had not yet adopted modern industrial technologies by the time an inflationary global monetary system began replacing a relatively sound one in 1914. This dysfunctional global monetary system continuously compromised these countries' development by enabling local and foreign governments to expropriate the wealth produced by their people."

In other words, rich countries got industrialized before they got fiat: Poor countries got fiat before they got industrialized. The only way to break the cycle of dependency, according to Nabourema and other organizers of the Africa Bitcoin Conference, might be to transcend fiat.

XVIII. A GLIMMER OF HOPE

"The root problem with conventional currency is all the trust that's required to make it work. The central bank must be trusted not to debase the currency, but the history of fiat currencies is full of breaches of that trust."

—*Satoshi Nakamoto*

Whatever the answer is to poverty in the Third World, we know it is not more debt. "The poor of the world," Cheryl Payer concludes, "don't need another 'bank,' however benign. They need decently paid work, responsive government, civil rights, and national autonomy."

For seven decades, the World Bank and IMF have been enemies of all four.

Looking forward, says Payer, "the most important task for those in the wealthy countries who are concerned with international solidarity is to actively fight to end the flow of foreign aid." The problem is that the current system is designed and incentivized to keep this flow going. The only way to make a change is through a total paradigm shift.

We already know that Bitcoin can help individuals inside developing countries gain personal financial freedom and escape the broken systems imposed on them by their corrupt rulers and international financial institutions. This is what was accelerated in Accra in December 2022, contra the designs of the World Bank and IMF. But can Bitcoin actually change the core periphery dynamics of the world's power and resource structure?

Farida Nabourema is hopeful, and doesn't understand why leftists in general condemn or ignore Bitcoin.

"A tool that is capable of allowing people to build and access wealth independent from institutions of control can be seen as a leftist project," she says. "As an activist that believes that citizens should be paid in currencies that actually value their life and sacrifices, Bitcoin is a people's revolution."

"I find it painful," she says, "that a farmer in sub-Saharan Africa only earns 1% of the price of coffee on the global market. If we can get to a stage where farmers can sell their coffee without so many middle institutions more directly to the buyers, and get paid in bitcoin, you could imagine how much of a difference that would make in their lives."

"Today," she says, "our countries in the Global South still borrow money in U.S. dollars, but over time our currencies depreciate and lose value and we end up having to make twice or three times the payment we initially promised in order to reimburse our creditors."

"Now imagine," she says, "if we get to a stage in ten or twenty years where bitcoin is the global money that is accepted for business worldwide, where every nation has to borrow in bitcoin and spend bitcoin and every nation has to pay their debts in bitcoin. In that world, then foreign governments cannot demand that we repay them in currencies that we need to earn but they can simply print; and just because they decide to increase their interest rates, it won't automatically jeopardize the lives of millions or billions of people in our countries."

"Of course," Nabourema says, "Bitcoin is going to come with issues like any innovation. But the beauty is that those issues can be improved with peaceful, global collaboration. No one knew twenty years ago what amazing things the internet allows us to do today. No one can tell what amazing things Bitcoin will allow us to do in twenty years."

"The way forward," she says, "is an awakening of the masses: for them to understand the ins and outs of how the system works and to understand that there are alternatives. We have to be in a position where people can reclaim their liberty, where their lives aren't controlled by authorities that can confiscate their freedom at any time without consequences. Gradually we are getting closer to this goal with Bitcoin."

"Since money is the center of everything in our world," Nabourema says, "the fact that we are now able to obtain financial independence is so important for people in our countries, as we seek to reclaim our rights in every field and sector."

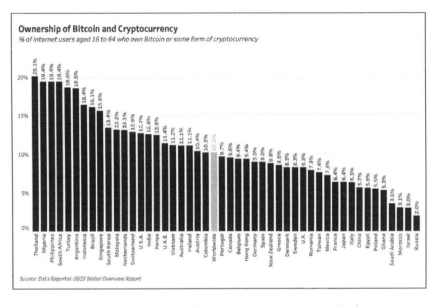

Bitcoin and cryptocurrency ownership per capita: countries with a history of IMF structural adjustments tend to rank very high.

Per the data, Bitcoin is already manifesting as a global reaction to World Bank and IMF policy. Thailand, Nigeria, the Philippines, Turkey, Argentina, Indonesia, and Brazil— who collectively entered loan agreements with the IMF a total of ninety-eight times and are historically some of the countries hit hardest by structural adjustment—rank as seven of the top-eight countries of the world in terms of Bitcoin and cryptocurrency usage per capita. Events like the Africa Bitcoin Conference, organized by activists trying to move beyond the Global South's neocolonial financial framework, will only contribute to this momentum.

For its part, the IMF appears to already view Bitcoin as a threat. In the spring of 2022, the Argentine government inked a new deal with the IMF where it promised to "discourage the use of cryptocurrencies."[228] The IMF has also repeatedly pushed back against El Salvador's Bitcoin adoption, urging the Nayib Bukele administration to sell its Bitcoin reserves and repeal its legal tender law. It's clear that the World Bank and the IMF will resist any change to the status quo.[229]

In an interview for this book, deflation advocate Jeff Booth explains that, as the world approaches a bitcoin standard, the World Bank and the IMF will be less likely to be creditors, and more likely to be co-investors, partners, or simply grantors. As prices fall over time, this means debt gets more expensive and more difficult to repay. With the U.S. money printer turned off, there would be no more bailouts. At first, he suggests, the World Bank and IMF will try to continue to lend, but for the first time, they'll actually lose big chunks of money as countries freely default as they move onto a bitcoin standard. So they may consider co-investing instead, where they might become more interested in the real success and sustainability of the projects they support as the risk is more equally shared.

Bitcoin mining is an additional area of potential change. If poor countries can exchange their natural resources for money without dealing with foreign powers, then maybe their sovereignty can strengthen instead of erode. Through mining, the vast amounts of river power, hydrocarbons, sun, wind, ground warmth, and offshore Ocean Thermal Energy Conversion (OTEC) in emerging markets could be converted

directly to the world reserve currency *without permission.*
This has never before been possible. The debt trap seems truly
inescapable for most poor countries, continuing to grow every
year. Maybe investing in anti-fiat Bitcoin reserves, services,
and infrastructure is a way out and a path to striking back.

Bitcoin, Booth says, can short-circuit the old system that
has subsidized wealthy countries at the expense of wages in
poor countries. In that old system, the periphery had to be
sacrificed to protect the core. In the new system, the periphery
and core can work together. Right now, he says, the U.S.
dollar system keeps people poor through wage deflation in the
periphery. But by equalizing the money and creating a neutral
standard for everyone, a different dynamic is created. With
one monetary standard, labor rates would be necessarily
pulled closer together instead of kept apart. We don't have
words for such a dynamic, Booth says, because it has never
existed: He suggests "forced cooperation."

A vivid example of this is how Bitcoin companies are
already saving people money as they try to send value from
the Global North to the Global South. Traditionally, American
or European firms would control this flow, and extract rent as
families and businesses sent value from, for example, New
York to Lagos. Despite the "street rate" of the Nigerian naira
being close to 750 per dollar in December 2022, a Western
Union–type wire would only net the recipient value at the
"official" rate of around 445 per dollar. But the Africa Bitcoin
Conference, a partnership was launched between the U.S.-
based Strike and the Nigeria-based Bitnob, where Americans
could send dollars arriving in minutes to Nigerian bank

accounts or Kenyan M-PESA mobile money accounts. Because the companies use Bitcoin's Lightning Network to speak to each other, the transfer nets the recipient the "street rate," saving as much as 40% in fees.

In 2023, the African continent has more than forty central banks, and none of the various African fiat currencies are interoperable. The system was not designed to unify and connect, but rather to divide and siphon value from citizens. In an open and permissionless Bitcoin model, it's easy to see how colonial borders and authoritarian corruption can begin to be overcome.

Booth describes the United States' ability to instantly issue any amount of more debt as "theft in base money." Readers may be familiar with the Cantillon effect, where those who are closest to the money printer benefit from fresh cash while those farthest away suffer. Well, it turns out there is a global Cantillon effect, too, where the United States benefits from issuing the global reserve currency, and poor countries suffer.

"A bitcoin standard," Booth says, "ends this."

How much of the world's debt is odious? There are *trillions* of dollars of loans created at the whim of dictators and unelected supranational financial institutions, with zero consent from the people on the borrowing side of the deal. The moral thing to do would be to cancel this debt, but of course, that will never happen because the loans exist ultimately as assets on the balance sheets of the creditors of the World Bank and IMF. They will always prefer to keep the assets and simply create new debt to pay the old.

The IMF "put" on sovereign debt creates the biggest bubble of all: bigger than the dot-com bubble, bigger than the subprime mortgage bubble, and bigger even than the stimulus-powered COVID-19 bubble. Unwinding this system will be extremely painful, but it's the right thing to do. If debt is the drug, and the World Bank and IMF are the dealers, and the developing country governments are the addicts, then it's unlikely either party will want to stop. But to heal, the addicts need to go to rehab. The fiat system makes this basically impossible. In the Bitcoin system, it may get to the point where the patient has no other choice.

As Saifedean Ammous says, if Brazil's rulers want to borrow $30 billion and the U.S. Congress agrees, America can snap its fingers and allocate the funds through the IMF. It's a political decision. But, he says, if we get rid of the money printer, then these decisions become less political and start to resemble the more prudent decision-making of a bank that knows no bailout will come.

In the last sixty years of World Bank and IMF dominance, countless tyrants and kleptocrats were bailed out—against any financial common sense—so that their nations' natural resources and labor could continue to be exploited by core countries. This was possible because the government at the very heart of the system could print the reserve currency.

But in a bitcoin standard, Ammous wonders, who is going to make these high risk, billion-dollar loans in exchange for structural adjustment?

"You," he asks, "and whose bitcoin?"

Recommended Reading

Ammous, Saifedean. *The Fiat Standard: The Debt Slavery Alternative to Human Civilization*. Pakistan: Saif House, 2021.

Ayittey, George. *Africa Betrayed*. New York: Palgrave Macmillan, 1992.

Ayittey, George. *Defeating Dictators: Fighting Tyranny in Africa and Around the World*. New York: St. Martin's Griffin, 2011.

Bandow, Douglas, and Ian Vàsquez, eds. *Perpetuating Poverty: The World Bank, the IMF, and the Developing World*. Washington, DC: CATO Institute, 1994.

Branford, Sue, and Bernando Kucinski. *The Debt Squads: The US, the Banks, and Latin America*. London, UK: Zed Books, 1988.

Burgis, Tom. *The Looting Machine: Warlords, Oligarchs, Corporations, Smugglers, and the Theft of Africa's Wealth*. New York: Public Affairs, 2016.

Copelovitch, Mark S. *The International Monetary Fund in the Global Economy: Banks, Bonds, and Bailouts*. London: Cambridge University Press, 2010.

Danaher, Kevin. *50 Years Is Enough: The Case Against the World Bank and the International Monetary Fund.* Boston, MA: South End Press, 1994.

Dreher, Axel, Andreas Fuchs, Bradley Parks, Austin Strange, and Michael J. Tierney. *Banking on Beijing: The Aims and Impacts of China's Overseas Development Program.* United Kingdom: Cambridge University Press, 2022.

Eich, Stefan. *The Currency of Politics: The Political Theory of Money from Aristotle to Keynes.* New Jersey: Princeton University Press, 2022.

George, Susan. *A Fate Worse than Debt: The World Financial Crisis and the Poor.* New York: Grove Press, 1990.

Graeber, David. *Debt: The First 5,000 Years.* Brooklyn, NY: Melville House, 2011.

Hancock, Graham. *The Lords of Poverty: The Power, Prestige, and Corruption of the International Aid Business.* New York: Atlantic Monthly Press, 1991.

Hickel, Jason, Dylan Sullivan, and Huzaifa Zoomkawala. "Plunder in the Post-Colonial Era: Quantifying Drain from the Global South Through Unequal Exchange, 1960–2018." *New Political Economy* 26, no. 6 (2021): p. 1030–1047.

Moyo, Dambisa. *Dead Aid: Why Aid Is Not Working and How There Is a Better Way for Africa.* New York: Farrar, Straus and Giroux, 2009.

Patnaik, Utsa, and Prabhat Patnaik. *Capital and Imperialism: Theory, History, and the Present*. New York: Monthly Review Press, 2021.

Payer, Cheryl. *The Debt Trap: The International Monetary Fund and the Third World*. New York: Monthly Review Press, 1975.

Payer, Cheryl. *Lent and Lost: Foreign Credit and Third World Development*. London, UK: Zed Books, 1991.

Payer, Cheryl. *The World Bank: A Critical Analysis*. New York: Monthly Review Press, 1982.

Perlez, Jane, & Raymond Bonner. "Below a Mountain of Wealth, a River of Waste." *New York Times*, December 27th, 2005, https://www.nytimes.com/2005/12/27/world/asia/below-a-mountain-of-wealth-a-river-of-waste.html.

Pigeaud, Fanny, and Ndongo Samba Sylla. *Africa's Last Colonial Currency: The CFA Franc Story*. London, UK: Pluto Press, 2021.

HOPE FOR THE COLONIZED

In the course of this book, Alex Gladstein demonstrates how Bretton Woods institutions, such as the IMF and the World Bank, have exacerbated poverty and spawned enormous environmental problems in the Global South, rendering the region's already impoverished population even more helpless and vulnerable.

This book takes us on a journey to discover the labyrinth of debts that increase the dependence of developing nations, which are frequently forced to accept loans to finance projects that benefit only a small elite and foreign corporations and institutions.

It is bizarre to see how this system has functioned for decades in various regions of the world, where the poor finance their own oppression without realizing that their governments contract loans with outrageously high interest rates that only serve low-income generating industries and businesses that are not profitable to the populations.

This book debunks the economic model imposed by the IMF and the World Bank on the basis of a narrative that is validated by the myth of economic growth as determined by exports.

Furthermore, the author demonstrates that the continuation of predatory economic systems is frequently only possible under autocratic regimes in which the populace has no ability to hold their leaders accountable for their poor decisions.

The debt system—as laid bare in the preceding pages—is a continuation of colonization that is even more pervasive, as the colonized borrow to finance their own oppression and are required to repay with interest. This time, the colonizers are no longer required to take any financial risks, as they will always receive a return that is vastly greater than their initial investment at almost no cost.

What Gladstein criticizes is not the mere fact that wealthy nations impose neoliberal policies on poorer ones by requiring them to create industries that are economically and environmentally ruinous for them, in addition to demanding free trade. While farmers in Africa, Asia, and Latin America no longer receive financial assistance from their governments to reduce public spending, as required by the IMF and the World Bank, farmers in wealthier nations frequently continue to receive government subsidies. He highlights the double standards by which subsidies are tolerated and accepted for wealthy nations while they are nearly eradicated in developing ones making the goods of developing nations less competitive.

Although Gladstein's book rages against the injustice that characterizes the neoliberal economic model and the Bretton Woods institutions, it ultimately offers a glimmer of hope by demonstrating how Bitcoin, with its liberating philosophy, decentralized technology, and immutable functionality, can help free nations and peoples from the debt trap.

Bitcoin will not magically erase centuries of financial exploitation, environmental destruction, and moral abyss, but it offers the world and especially the populations of countries impoverished by the insatiable greed of their leaders and foreign institutions like the IMF and the World Bank, a chance to break free.

—Farida Nabourema

Togolese writer,
human rights defender,
and Pan-Africanist

About the Author

Alex Gladstein is the chief strategy officer at the Human Rights Foundation. He has also served as vice president of strategy for the Oslo Freedom Forum since its inception in 2009. In his work, Alex has connected hundreds of dissidents and civil society groups with business leaders, technologists, journalists, philanthropists, policymakers, and artists to promote free and open societies.

Alex's writing and views on human rights and technology have appeared in media outlets across the world including *The Atlantic*, BBC, CNN, *The Guardian*, *Foreign Policy*, *The New York Times*, NPR, *TIME*, *The Washington Post*, *WIRED*, and *The Wall Street Journal*. He has spoken at universities ranging from MIT to Stanford, briefed the European Parliament and US State Department, and serves as faculty at Singularity University and as an advisor to Blockchain Capital, a leading venture firm in the fintech industry.

He frequently speaks and writes about why Bitcoin matters for freedom. Alex is co-author of *The Little Bitcoin Book* (2019), author of *Check Your Financial Privilege* (2022), and a regular contributor to *Bitcoin Magazine*.

ENDNOTES

[1] https://www.preventionweb.net/blog/whats-changed-1970-great-bhola-cyclone

[2] https://en.wikipedia.org/wiki/1970_Bhola_cyclone

[3] https://water104website.weebly.com/bangladesh-flooding-and-impacts.html

[4] https://www.nationalgeographic.com/environment/article/climate-change-drives-migration-crisis-in-bangladesh-from-dhaka-sundabans

[5] http://madadoc.irenala.edu.mg/documents/9353_Shrimp%20report-WorldBank.pdf

[6] https://www.imf.org/external/np/fin/tad/extarr2.aspx?memberKey1=55&date1key=2013-11-30

[7] https://puccifoods.com/hidden-human-cost-part-1-abuse-injustice-bangladesh-shrimp-farming-industry/

[8] http://madadoc.irenala.edu.mg/documents/9353_Shrimp%20report-WorldBank.pdf

[9] https://whc.unesco.org/en/list/798/

[10] https://www.wrm.org.uy/bulletin-articles/bangladesh-losing-mangroves-to-shrimp-farming-leads-to-food-loss-and-environmental-insecurity

[11] https://ejfoundation.org/resources/downloads/desert_in_the_delta.pdf

[12] https://www.cdpbd.org/images/files/Working%20together%20for%20eco-friendly%20responsible%20shrimp%20farming.pdf

[13] https://aquafishcrsp.oregonstate.edu/biblio/threatening-white-gold-impacts-climate-change-shrimp-farming-coastal-bangladesh

[14] https://www.cdpbd.org/images/files/Working%20together%20for%20eco-friendly%20responsible%20shrimp%20farming.pdf

[15] https://www.reuters.com/article/bangladesh-shrimp/bangladeshis-exploited-so-west-can-eat-cheap-shrimp-report-idINDEEA0K0EH20140121

[16] https://www.cdpbd.org/images/files/Working%20together%20for%20eco-friendly%20responsible%20shrimp%20farming.pdf

[17] https://ejfoundation.org/resources/downloads/desert_in_the_delta.pdf

[18] https://www.researchgate.net/publication/225513242_Economic_returns_of_disease_extensive_shrimp_farming_in_southwest_Bangladesh

[19] https://ejfoundation.org/resources/downloads/desert_in_the_delta.pdf

[20] https://www.thethirdpole.net/en/livelihoods/bangladeshs-shrimp-industry-drives-freshwater-crisis/

[21] https://www.sciencedaily.com/releases/2009/04/090414172924.htm

22 https://www.worldbank.org/en/results/2022/08/24/helping-bangladish-protect-its-coastal-communities-from-tidal-flooding-and-storm-surges
23 https://www.citizen.org/article/world-banks-destructive-policies-about-shrimp-farming-endanger-communities-in-developing-countries/
24 https://www.worldbank.org/en/news/press-release/2022/05/23/world-bank-support-for-the-development-of-morocco-s-blue-economy
25 https://base.d-p-h.info/en/fiches/prcmierdph/fiche-premierdph-4016.html
26 https://www.worldbank.org/en/country/bangladesh/overview
27 https://www.imf.org/external/np/fin/tad/extarr2.aspx?memberKey1=55&date1key=2013-11-30
28 https://www.macrotrends.net/countries/BGD/bangladesh/external-debt-stock
29 https://www.ceicdata.com/en/indicator/bangladesh/external-debt
30 https://www.imf.org/en/News/Articles/2022/11/08/pr22375-bangladesh
31 https://www.belfercenter.org/sites/default/files/legacy/files/the_american_campaign_for_environmental_reforms_at_the_world_bank.pdf
32 https://www.worldbank.org/en/who-we-are/ibrd
33 https://www.imf.org/external/pubs/ft/ar/archive/pdf/ar1965.pdf
34 https://www.worldbank.org/en/archive/history/exhibits/Bretton-Woods-and-the-Birth-of-the-World-Bank
35 https://www.imf.org/external/np/sec/memdir/memdate.htm
36 https://www.imf.org/external/np/fin/data/rms_sdrv.aspx
37 https://www.cnbc.com/2020/03/16/imf-says-its-ready-to-mobilize-its-1-trillion-lending-capacity-to-fight-coronavirus.html
38 https://www.worldbank.org/en/about/history/the-world-bank-group-and-the-imf
39 https://inquiries.worldbank.org/knowledgebase/articles/931722-miga
40 https://www.amazon.com/World-Bank-Critical-Analysis-Monthly/dp/085345602X
41 https://www.worldbank.org/en/about/leadership/votingpowers
42 https://www.imf.org/en/About/executive-board/members-quotas
43 https://www.amazon.com/International-Monetary-Fund-Global-Economy/dp/0521194334
44 https://www.imf.org/en/About/infographics/imf-firepower-lending
45 https://www.worldbank.org/en/news/press-release/2022/08/08/world-bank-group-releases-fy22-audited-financial-statements
46 https://www.oxfam.org/en/international-financial-institutions/imf-covid-19-financing-and-fiscal-tracker

[47] https://www.worldbank.org/en/news/press-release/2021/07/19/world-bank-group-s-157-billion-pandemic-surge-is-largest-crisis-response-in-its-history
[48] https://www.imf.org/en/About/FAQ/imf-response-to-covid-19
[49] https://www.amnesty.org/en/latest/press-release/2019/08/egypt-bitter-legacy-of-rabaa-massacre-continues-to-haunt-egyptians/
[50] https://arabcenterdc.org/resource/egypt-and-the-imf-greater-foreign-debt-and-deeper-economic-decline/
[51] https://www.reuters.com/world/africa/ethiopia-world-bank-sign-300-mln-grant-agreement-reconstruction-2022-05-17/
[52] https://www.thenation.com/article/world/genocide-in-tigray/
[53] https://www.amazon.com/Lords-Poverty-Prestige-Corruption-International/dp/0871134691
[54] https://www.amazon.com/Lent-Lost-Foreign-Credit-Development/dp/0862329531
[55] https://www.worldometers.info/world-population/world-population-by-year
[56] https://projects.worldbank.org/en/projects-operations/project-country?lang=en&page=
[57] https://www.ft.com/content/eab481e5-9841-43a5-a072-f09124e7167d
[58] https://www.wsj.com/livecoverage/stock-market-news-today-11-23-2022/card/ghana-plans-debt-exchange-as-economic-crisis-mounts-HCIOCltDEPELXPNx7E7u
[59] https://www.elibrary.imf.org/display/book/9781557753021/ch05.xml?language=en
[60] https://www.amazon.com/Cheryl-Payer/e/B001KIKTLQ%3Fref=dbs_a_mng_rwt_scns_share
[61] https://www.amazon.com/Debt-Trap-International-Monetary-Monthly/dp/0853453764
[62] https://www.cfr.org/backgrounder/imf-worlds-controversial-financial-firefighter?amp
[63] https://www.cambridge.org/core/books/human-rights-and-structural-adjustment/8FDF11EE5647374B8F9FD50A18570AD3
[64] https://www.amazon.com/Debt-Trap-International-Monetary-Monthly/dp/0853453764
[65] https://www.amazon.com/Debt-Trap-International-Monetary-Monthly/dp/0853453764
[66] https://www.amazon.com/World-Bank-Critical-Analysis-Monthly/dp/085345602X
[67] https://en.wikipedia.org/wiki/Washington_Consensus
[68] https://bitcoinmagazinc.com/culture/bitcoin-a-currency-of-decolonization

[69] https://www.nytimes.com/1994/02/23/world/french-devaluation-of-african-currency-brings-wide-unrest.html

[70] https://www.imf.org/external/pubs/ft/fabric/backgrnd.htm

[71] https://www.amazon.com/International-Monetary-Fund-Global-Economy/dp/0521194334

[72] https://www.amazon.com/International-Monetary-Fund-Global-Economy/dp/0521194334

[73] https://www.reuters.com/article/us-imf-conditions/imf-loan-conditions-grow-despite-vows-to-limit-them-study-idUSBREA311SZ20140402

[74] https://www.reuters.com/article/us-imf-conditions/imf-loan-conditions-grow-despite-vows-to-limit-them-study-idUSBREA311SZ20140402

[75] https://www.worldbank.org/en/archive/history

[76] https://www.tandfonline.com/doi/abs/10.1080/13563467.2021.1899153

[77] https://www.amazon.com/Debt-IMF-World-Bank-Questions/dp/1583672222

[78] https://amp.theguardian.com/global-development-professionals-network/2017/jan/14/aid-in-reverse-how-poor-countries-develop-rich-countries

[79] https://amp.theguardian.com/global-development-professionals-network/2017/jan/14/aid-in-reverse-how-poor-countries-develop-rich-countries

[80] https://www.tandfonline.com/doi/full/10.1080/13563467.2021.1899153

[81] https://www.tandfonline.com/doi/full/10.1080/13563467.2021.1899153

[82] https://www.worldbank.org/en/news/press-release/2021/10/11/low-income-country-debt-rises-to-record-860-billion-in-2020

[83] https://amp.theguardian.com/global-development-professionals-network/2017/jan/14/aid-in-reverse-how-poor-countries-develop-rich-countries

[84] https://www.bloomberg.com/news/articles/2023-01-05/debt-payments-consume-80-of-nigeria-s-revenue-collection

[85] https://www.amazon.com/Debt-Trap-International-Monetary-Monthly/dp/0853453764

[86] https://www.tandfonline.com/doi/full/10.1080/13563467.2021.1899153

[87] https://www.tandfonline.com/doi/full/10.1080/13563467.2021.1899153

[88] https://aeon.co/essays/if-you-want-decolonisation-go-to-the-economics-of-samir-amin

[89] https://www.tandfonline.com/doi/full/10.1080/13563467.2021.1899153

[90] https://www.wider.unu.edu/sites/default/files/Publications/Book/Book-commodites-crisis.pdf

[91] https://books.google.com/books/about/50_Years_is_Enough.html?id=XK6Egbw4-PcC

[92] https://www.tandfonline.com/doi/full/10.1080/13563467.2021.1899153

[93] https://documents1.worldbank.org/curated/en/240201586262870698/pdf/Announcement-of-Loan-Granted-to-Southern-Rhodesia-on-February-27-1952.pdf

[94] https://www.imf.org/external/np/fin/tad/extarr2.aspx?memberKey1=280&date1key=2017-04-30

[95] https://www.newyorker.com/magazine/1993/12/06/the-truth-of-el-mozote

[96] https://publicintegrity.org/accountability/leaked-report-says-world-bank-violated-own-rules-in-ethiopia/

[97] https://projects.huffingtonpost.com/projects/worldbank-evicted-abandoned/new-evidence-ties-worldbank-to-human-rights-abuses-ethiopia

[98] https://www.imf.org/external/np/fin/tad/extarr2.aspx?memberKey1=197&date1key=2002-06-30

[99] https://peri.umass.edu/images/Congo_s_Odious_Debts.pdf

[100] https://www.latimes.com/archives/la-xpm-1997-05-17-mn-59626-story.html

[101] https://www.brookings.edu/research/odious-debt/

[102] https://www.imf.org/external/pubs/ft/fandd/2002/06/kremer.htm

[103] https://www.marxists.org/archive/sankara/1987/july/29.htm

[104] https://www.cfr.org/article/what-sankara-assassination-trial-means-west-africa

[105] https://www.imf.org/external/np/fin/tad/extarr2.aspx?memberKey1=95&date1key=2002-06-30

[106] https://projects.worldbank.org/en/projects-operations/projects-list?lang=en&countrycode_exact=BF&os=100&countryshortname_exact=Burkina%20Faso

[107] https://www.phenomenalworld.org/analysis/odious-debts/

[108] https://www.npr.org/sections/money/2022/03/22/1087654279/how-shock-therapy-created-russian-oligarchs-and-paved-the-path-for-putin

[109] https://www.heritage.org/europe/report/russias-meltdown-anatomy-the-imf-failure

[110] https://star.worldbank.org/deauville-partnership-arab-countries-transition

[111] https://www.theguardian.com/commentisfree/2018/jan/17/imf-tunisia-people-rioting-2011-economic-reforms

[112] http://www.economie-tunisie.org/sites/default/files/fmi_impact_of_tunisias_currency_devaluation_en.pdf

[113] https://tradingeconomics.com/commodity/wheat

[114] https://www.reuters.com/markets/asia/pakistan-imf-begin-talks-7-bln-loan-review-2022-11-28/

[115] https://www.imf.org/en/News/Articles/2022/09/01/pr22295-imf-reaches-staff-level-agreement-on-an-extended-fund-facility-arrangement-with-sri-lanka

[116] https://www.imf.org/en/News/Articles/2022/10/26/pr22363-egypt-imf-reaches-staff-level-agreement-on-an-extended-fund-facility-arrangement

[117] https://www.imf.org/en/News/Articles/2022/10/20/pr22363-imf-staff-statement-on-ghana

[118] https://www.imf.org/en/News/Articles/2022/11/08/pr22375-bangladesh

[119] https://www.amazon.com/World-Bank-Critical-Analysis-Monthly/dp/085345602X

[120] https://www.amazon.com/Fate-Worse-Than-Debt/dp/0802131212

[121] https://www.amazon.com/Debt-Squads-Banks-Latin-America/dp/0862327911

[122] https://tradingeconomics.com/niger/exports

[123] https://tradingeconomics.com/mali/exports

[124] https://tradingeconomics.com/zambia/exports

[125] https://tradingeconomics.com/burundi/exports

[126] https://tradingeconomics.com/malawi/exports

[127] https://tradingeconomics.com/togo/exports

[128] https://www.amazon.com/Debt-IMF-World-Bank-Questions/dp/1583672222

[129] https://www.amazon.com/World-Bank-Critical-Analysis-Monthly/dp/085345602X

[130] https://www.nobelprize.org/prizes/peace/1970/borlaug/biographical/

[131] https://unctad.org/news/covid-19-threat-food-security-africa

[132] https://www.brookings.edu/blog/africa-in-focus/2020/12/14/unpacking-the-misconceptions-about-africas-food-imports/

[133] https://en.wikipedia.org/wiki/1985_Mexico_City_earthquake

[134] https://newint.org/features/1979/11/01/modernisation-game

[135] https://en.wikipedia.org/wiki/Patrice_Talon

[136] http://shores-system.mysite.com/development_set.html

[137] https://www.forbes.com/sites/robertwood/2012/05/30/imfs-christine-lagarde-i-dont-pay-taxes-but-you-should/?sh=1dad4c877cbd

[138] https://www.amazon.com/Debt-IMF-World-Bank-Questions/dp/1583672222

[139] https://www.amazon.com/Globalization-Its-Discontents-Norton-Paperback/dp/0393324397

[140] https://www.worldbank.org/en/archive/history/past-presidents/robert-strange-mcnamara

[141] https://www.nytimes.com/2021/06/09/us/pentagon-papers-vietnam-war.html
[142] https://www.imf.org/en/Publications/Books/Issues/2016/12/30/Balance-of-Payments-Adjustment-1945-to-1986-The-IMF-Experience-21
[143] https://www.amazon.com/Lent-Lost-Foreign-Credit-Development/dp/0862329531
[144] https://en.wikipedia.org/wiki/Inga_dams
[145] http://www.columbia.edu/itc/sipa/martin/chad-cam/overview.html
[146] https://openknowledge.worldbank.org/bitstream/handle/10986/3118/AAA420ESW0WHIT110papureport1english.pdf?sequence=1&isAllowed=y
[147] https://png.wcs.org/Wildlife/Corals.aspx
[148] https://en.wikipedia.org/wiki/Indonesian_National_Revolution
[149] https://www.jstor.org/stable/2644481
[150] https://link.springer.com/article/10.1007/s002679900049
[151] https://www.aljazeera.com/opinions/2011/10/19/west-papua-a-history-of-exploitation
[152] http://wpik.org/Src/NYT/19590306newExplor.pdf
[153] https://www.nytimes.com/2005/12/27/world/asia/below-a-mountain-of-wealth-a-river-of-waste.html
[154] https://en.wikipedia.org/wiki/Lorentz_National_Park
[155] https://www.tapol.org/sites/default/files/sites/default/files/pdfs/PT_Freeport_Indo_tail_of_violations_in_Papua_Dec20.pdf
[156] https://openknowledge.worldbank.org/bitstream/handle/10986/3118/AAA420ESW0WHIT110papureport1english.pdf?sequence=1&isAllowed=y
[157] https://www.nadir.org/nadir/initiativ/agp/free/imf/asia/papua.htm
[158] https://link.springer.com/article/10.1007/s002679900049
[159] https://www.tapol.org/sites/default/files/sites/default/files/pdfs/West_Papua_2021_Freedom_of_Expression_Assembly_Report.pdf
[160] https://www.amnesty.org/en/latest/news/2022/03/indonesia-gold-mine-papua/
[161] https://documents1.worldbank.org/curated/en/451151468269127930/text/multi-page.txt
[162] https://link.springer.com/article/10.1007/s002679900049
[163] https://www.theguardian.com/global-development/2016/nov/02/100-bn-dollar-gold-mine-west-papuans-say-they-are-counting-the-cost-indonesia
[164] https://link.springer.com/article/10.1007/s002679900049
[165] http://web.worldbank.org/archive/website00903F/WEB/PDF/PR121101

.PDF
[166] https://archive.nytimes.com/www.nytimes.com/cwire/2009/08/19/19climatewire-how-the-world-bank-let-deal-making-torch-the-33255.html
[167] https://projects.worldbank.org/en/projects-operations/project-detail/P040578
[168] https://www.nber.org/system/files/working_papers/w21805/w21805.pdf
[169] https://www.imf.org/en/Publications/Books/Issues/2016/12/30/Balance-of-Payments-Adjustment-1945-to-1986-The-IMF-Experience-21
[170] https://www.amazon.com/International-Monetary-Fund-Global-Economy/dp/0521194334
[171] https://www.tni.org/en/article/a-fate-worse-than-debt-the-world-financial-crisis-and-the-poor
[172] https://www.imf.org/external/np/fin/tad/extarr2.aspx?memberKey1=30&date1key=2019-08-31
[173] https://www.theguardian.com/world/2018/sep/26/argentina-imf-biggest-loan
[174] https://www.commonwealthfund.org/international-health-policy-center/countries/england
[175] https://www.usda.gov/topics/farming/resources-small-and-mid-sized-farmers
[176] https://www.imf.org/en/Publications/Books/Issues/2016/12/30/Balance-of-Payments-Adjustment-1945-to-1986-The-IMF-Experience-21
[177] https://academic.oup.com/book/26536/chapter-abstract/195055373?redirectedFrom=fulltext
[178] https://en.wikipedia.org/wiki/Interest_Equalization_Tax
[179] https://www.rba.gov.au/education/resources/explainers/the-global-financial-crisis.html
[180] https://www.imf.org/external/np/exr/ib/2000/062300.htm
[181] https://www.bloomberg.com/news/articles/2022-09-28/us-treasury-is-alarmed-at-the-uk-economic-chaos-unleashed-by-liz-truss
[182] https://www.imf.org/en/About/Factsheets/Sheets/2022/Gold-in-the-IMF
[183] https://www.history.com/this-day-in-history/fdr-takes-united-states-off-gold-standard
[184] https://unfccc.int/cop27
[185] https://www.thenationalnews.com/arts-culture/books/the-story-of-pakistan-s-improbable-pursuit-of-nuclear-weapons-1.581758
[186] https://muse.jhu.edu/pub/1/monograph/chapter/3049886/pdf
[187] https://www.forbes.com/sites/michaelshellenberger/2022/09/22/haiti-riots-triggered-by-imf-advice-to-cut-fuel-subsidies/?sh=3qf8be9b5169

[188] https://www.downtoearth.org.in/blog/mcnamara-shoots-from-the-hip-29861

[189] https://newint.org/features/2022/12/05/neoliberalism-16-million-and-counting-collateral-damage-capital

[190] https://www.sciencedirect.com/science/article/pii/S0305750X22002169

[191] https://journals.sagepub.com/doi/abs/10.1177/1086026611413931?journalCode=oaec

[192] https://www.ncbi.nlm.nih.gov/pmc/articles/PMC5810102/

[193] https://www.sciencedirect.com/science/article/pii/S0277953619304897

[194] https://www.medrxiv.org/content/10.1101/2021.03.12.21253458v1.full

[195] https://www.jstor.org/stable/25790017

[196] https://gh.bmj.com/content/bmjgh/8/2/e011620.full.pdf

[197] https://www.imf.org/en/About/Factsheets/Sheets/2016/08/01/16/11/Debt-Relief-Under-the-Heavily-Indebted-Poor-Countries-Initiative

[198] https://www.npr.org/sections/goatsandsoda/2015/04/17/399816448/when-the-world-bank-does-more-harm-than-good

[199] https://www.nber.org/system/files/working_papers/w21805/w21805.pdf

[200] https://www.nytimes.com/2018/06/19/business/economy/greece-europe-bailout.html

[201] https://www.cfr.org/backgrounder/imf-worlds-controversial-financial-firefighter?amp

[202] https://www.worldbank.org/en/news/press-release/2021/07/19/world-bank-group-s-157-billion-pandemic-surge-is-largest-crisis-response-in-its-history

[203] https://www.jstor.org/stable/29790240

[204] https://www.cfr.org/backgrounder/chinas-massive-belt-and-road-initiative

[205] https://www.project-syndicate.org/commentary/china-one-belt-one-road-loans-debt-by-brahma-chellaney-2017-01

[206] https://www.devex.com/news/china-is-owed-37-of-poor-countries-debt-payments-in-2022-world-bank-102463

[207] https://open.spotify.com/episode/5Dq0ONxhBxuHS4e5nlbhAu?si=013bVmFgSD-qOXdVxvghQ&context=spotify:show:5REGIacamp72nJvZIUzn2q&nd=1

[208] https://www.bu.edu/gdp/2021/03/08/bailouts-from-beijing-how-china-functions-as-an-alternative-to-the-imf/

[209] https://chinaglobalsouth.com/2022/10/31/china-based-development-bank-to-ramp-up-lending-by-10-billion-a-year/

[210] https://open.spotify.com/episode/5Dq0ONxhBxuHS4e5nlbhAu?
si=013bVmFgSD-_qOXdVxvghQ&context=spotify:show:5REGIacamp72nJv
ZIUzn2q&nd=1

[211] https://www.rfa.org/english/news/myanmar/rareearths-
08092022183340.html

[212] https://www.orfonline.org/expert-speak/chinas-scramble-for-africas-
rare-earth-elements/

[213] https://en.wikipedia.org/wiki/Arusha_Declaration

[214] https://press.princeton.edu/books/hardcover/9780691191072/the-
currency-of-politics

[215] https://journals.sagepub.com/doi/abs/10.1177/030639688802900303?
journalCode=racb

[216] https://data.worldbank.org/indicator/DT.ODA.ODAT.CD?locations=
GH

[217] https://therealnews.com/ghanas-unions-and-left-reject-bailout-talks-
with-the-imf-as-economic-crisis-spirals

[218] https://www.bloomberg.com/news/articles/2022-11-10/cedi-s-drop-
for-months-portends-deeper-losses-for-ghana-currency

[219] https://www.nytimes.com/1978/05/09/archives/cia-said-to-have-
aided-plotters-who-overthrew-nkrumah-in-ghana.html

[220] https://www.ft.com/content/2cffb07c-828c-400d-a51a-2c52a00bb8e0

[221] https://www.macrotrends.net/countries/GHA/ghana/external-debt-
stock

[222] https://www.afrobitcoin.org

[223] https://twitter.com/gladstein/status/1599704740392501248

[224] https://twitter.com/gladstein/status/1599708581439635459?s=20&t=
VIvQ0QMfhVUTgLwinVBcsQ

[225] https://en.wikipedia.org/wiki/Dependency_theory

[226] https://www.tandfonline.com/doi/abs/10.1080/08935698808657801
?journalCode=rrmx20

[227] https://allenfarrington.medium.com/this-is-not-capitalism-
5ed0a9d5dfa9

[228] https://www.coindesk.com/policy/2022/03/18/argentine-congress-
approves-imf-debt-deal-that-would-discourage-crypto-usage/

[229] https://www.pbs.org/newshour/economy/imf-urges-el-salvador-to-
scale-back-its-push-for-bitcoin-as-legal-tender

Printed in Poland
by Amazon Fulfillment
Poland Sp. z o.o., Wrocław
09 May 2023

18d080fd-1549-4478-a540-a0b828c14d8bR02